# PETER CALLAHAN'S PARTY FOOD

# Peter Callahan's

# PARTY FOOD

*Mini Hors d'Oeuvres • Family-Style Settings • Plated Dishes*
*Buffet Spreads • Bar Carts*

Clarkson Potter/Publishers
New York

*To my wonderful wife, Josephine,
who is my partner in all things*

# CONTENTS

# Foreword

I first met Peter when he had just come up with his concept for shrinking comfort food into small, single bites to serve at parties. That was almost twenty years ago.

These were perfect for my fashion events, where we wanted things that were cute and fun, but also easy to eat. Not long after, Peter started pairing mini drinks with his mini foods and those became my next must-haves.

All these things Peter did first, but what many people may not be aware of is that Peter interprets ideas across the whole party spectrum, including buffets, seated dinners, carts and more. He understands people and their vision for entertaining.

A beach vacation in Mexico influenced the planning for my husband Andy's birthday. I told Peter I wanted shanty chic food and displays—I said I wanted mismatched flatware that looked like it had been run over by a truck as an analogy for the whole feel of the party. Peter so got it and carried that concept throughout the event. It felt authentic and completely captured the mood I wanted.

Peter's hors d'oeuvres are legendary and, as you can see in this book, he keeps ringing up hit after hit, but it's the treatment of all the components of food and beverage where his genius continues to shine. It may be shanty-chic Mexican for a birthday or a fine French multi-course dinner for a European crowd, but guests at either event will enjoy delicious food, even if their number is in the hundreds.

And then there are all the other aspects of an event that he creates, all these innovative serving displays—like a cake made of caviar (page 17), served at a special occasion instead of dessert, or carving stations for fish or meat that look like art (pages 28–29, 40–41) but are practical and function well to serve your guests.

It is often said by others that there is nothing new in the world of design and parties, but Peter proves year in and year out that he has a treasure trove of unique and appealing ideas to amaze and delight us all.

I am so thankful that he has pulled the curtain back to share his knowledge. Consider it your invitation to the world of Peter's parties.

*Kate Spade*

# Introduction

The press has called me "the king of hors d'oeuvres," and it's true that I may be most well known for introducing the world to mini comfort food, often with matching mini drinks, served on custom-designed trays. So it was natural that my first book, *Bite by Bite*, focused on these concepts.

But I dream up ideas across the entire landscape of the event world: platter layouts and structures for buffets that are simple yet original, creative serving carts for drinks, and beautiful designs for plates of delicious, seasonal food.

I work with clients who dine at the best restaurants around the world and wish to replicate such experiences for their own landmark celebrations, such as a three-hundred-guest wedding or thousand-person charity dinner. So we at Peter Callahan have become experts in creating perfect meals that look and taste amazing and can be served quickly to hundreds of people.

When I do my job correctly, it brings great joy to those who attend these parties—and the work that goes on behind the scenes is invisible to them. But I would like more of the public to be able to experience what I do without having to hire me. So now I am pulling back the curtain on my culinary design world.

When my team and I think of a new idea, our first thought is: Can we do this for a large group of people? We have the advantage of working from what used to be Jive Records recording studio, and is now our seven-thousand-square-foot kitchen and design studio, in New York City's Chelsea neighborhood. Close to thirty employees work in our space daily. But then we pack up everything needed for the event and ship it all off in trucks—and sometimes planes—to an event site that usually has no kitchen. From there, we serve hundreds of guests, perhaps even a thousand, according to precise timelines.

But no matter the size of the event, we take the same approach: Can we create something beautiful and fresh and elegant and perhaps entertaining that, to our knowledge, hasn't been done before? Can we create something that is personal to our hosts or unique to the environment of the event?

We always set out to see how we can do things in a different way; we rethink every part of the food and beverage experience at each event. It is this approach that defines us and differentiates us as caterers and event planners.

But the same steps we take in designing a large-scale event are ones you can follow at home, allowing you to serve dinner and then enjoy it along with your guests. Our criteria for dishes that can be put together easily at the last minute, with a lot of the prep done ahead, are perhaps even more beneficial for the home cook who doesn't have helpers in the kitchen.

This book contains the best of our ideas. Luckily, they just keep rolling in, and it is this continuing creative process that makes our business a joy. Here, we open our kitchen to share far and wide the ideas that our clients have relished the most and to help you translate them for a variety of situations.

Enjoy!

*Peter*

# Kitchen Tools and Conveniences

The recipes in this book will result in delicious food, but the dishes are made that much more special by their presentation. Let's discuss the equipment that will not only make the food preparation easier but also help you achieve the right look.

## Baking Dishes

Whether glass, ceramic, or stainless steel, baking dishes are inexpensive and very useful for everything from marinating to baking to serving to storing. Stock your cabinets with an assortment of sizes, including 8 and 9 inches square and 9 × 11- and 9 × 13-inch oblongs.

## Baking Sheets

Rimmed baking sheets measuring 18 × 13 inches, also known as half-sheet pans, are a necessity. Quarter-sheets (9 × 13 inches) are useful, too. It's good to have at least two of each size.

## Blender

A good blender with a tight-fitting lid is a kitchen basic that can puree anything from soup to frozen fruit for smoothies and cocktails. If you don't have one, or are looking to buy a new one, consider a high-speed model like a Vitamix. This will crush ice easily, perfectly emulsify homemade mayonnaise and other sauces, make flour from whole nuts, and extract fresh juices from whole fruits and vegetables.

## Cast-Iron Skillet

You can cook, bake, or sear just about anything in a cast-iron skillet, but what it does best is fry. The cast iron heats evenly and keeps the oil at a steady temperature. Buy a deep skillet (at least 5 inches high) with a lid—it's especially great for recipes like Mini Chicken Wings (page 63), Eggplant Meatballs (page 65), Homemade Potato Chips (page 43), and Breakfast Egg Rolls (page 74). Cast-iron skillets are inexpensive, too, so it won't break the budget to get one—or two.

## Cocktail Shaker

For mixing margaritas and martinis in style.

## Cookie Cutters

Start collecting biscuit or cookie cutters in lots of fun shapes and assorted sizes, from standard round and square ones to specialty shapes like pigs, musical notes, and bones.

## Cups and Glasses

Cordial glasses, mini tulip glasses, sake cups, silver mint julep cups, mini beer steins, espresso cups, and small shot glasses are incredibly versatile. Use them for drinks, cocktails, soups, and even for some desserts.

## Dishers

In addition to the ice cream scoop you know and love, dishers come in a wide range of sizes that make it easy to create consistently sized portions. We frequently use a #100 disher, which holds ¾ tablespoon, for hors d'oeuvres like our Eggplant Meatballs (page 65) and Meatballs (page 37). Larger versions that hold up to ⅓ cup are available, and you can even find an oval-shaped disher that makes attractive quenelles of sorbet (see page 181).

## Fine-Mesh Sieve

A medium to large fine-mesh sieve is great for straining everything from cereal milk (see page 94) to Sorrel Soup (page 115). You can also use it as a pasta strainer instead of a colander.

## Food Processor

A kitchen workhorse for soups, sauces, purees, even cracker dough. Buying a model that includes a smaller work bowl is a great idea—it comes in handy as a spice grinder or for finely chopping nuts and herbs, making pastes, and processing foods in small batches.

## Grill Pans

I call for nonstick ridged and flat grill pans throughout the book. Ridged pans are great for getting grill marks on baby corn (see page 25), lemons (see page 198), and vegetables (see page 146). A flat grill pan, or griddle, makes cooking pancakes a breeze.

## Hotel Pans

Hotel pans are rectangular stainless steel pans used to cook, store, and serve food. Designed to fit into steam tables, they're great for marinating meat (see pages 152, 145, and 213), freezing granitas, and a host of other uses. A full-size hotel pan is about 12 × 20 inches and comes in 2-, 4-, and 6-inch depths. Half hotel pans, which are about 12 × 10 inches, are nice for a smaller number of servings.

## Instant-Read Digital Thermometer

This is indispensable when knowing exact temperature is important—such as whether oil is hot enough for frying or meat is cooked to your liking. The kind with the probe attached to a base via a metal wire can be helpful—you can leave the probe in a pot of oil or in meat while it's in the oven. Some models also have an alarm to let you know when the oil is too hot or when your meat is perfectly cooked.

### Knives

You don't need any special knives to make the dishes in this book, although keeping your knives sharp and honed will make precision work easier. A chef's knife, paring knife, boning knife, serrated bread knife, and kitchen shears are the essentials.

### Mandoline

When you need super thin slices of potatoes (see pages 43 and 206), beets, and other vegetables, a mandoline makes the job a cinch.

### Microplane Grater

A can't-live-without tool for perfectly removing zest (and leaving the bitter pith behind) from citrus. Unlike a zester or a box grater, a Microplane removes zest in small bits, so there's no need to chop it into smaller pieces afterward.

### Mixing Bowls

Amass as many as your cupboards can handle! Small mixing bowls, especially stylish ones, can double as serving dishes for nuts or other small finger foods.

### Pastry Brush

A traditional pastry brush, silicone brush, or even small natural-bristle paintbrush from the hardware store is great for moistening the edges of wontons when sealing them, for brushing egg wash on pastry to give it a nice shine before it goes into the oven, or for brushing melted butter or olive oil onto vegetables before and after cooking.

### Pastry Tips

In addition to piping frostings or garnishes, I use pastry tips for everything from cutting out mini circles of mozzarella cheese (see page 57) to molding mini breads and ice cream cones (see pages 25 and 95).

### Pitchers and Carafes

Glass pitchers, vintage carafes, and decanters all work nicely for serving cocktails and mixers as well as nonalcoholic beverages.

### Platters and Trays

How else are you going to serve your beautiful creations? Always keep an eye out for cake plates, tiered hors d'oeuvre stands, platters, and trays of all sizes. I like white platters with clean lines, but if your style is all about French country, then choose colors and shapes that work with your decor and taste. Mixing a few neutral-colored platters into any collection is a good idea.

### Rolling Pin

Whether rolling out dough or flattening bread to make bread cones, a tapered French pin is lightweight and beautiful, and works like a charm.

### Ruler

A clear plastic ruler is easy to store and wash. A mini retractable tape measure comes in handy, too.

### Skillets and Sauté Pans

Nonstick and regular stainless steel skillets (or frying pans) have slanted sides, which make them perfect for quick cooking; sauté pans have straight sides and a larger surface area, so they're good for searing meat and reducing sauces.

### Slotted Spoon and Frying Spider

These utensils come in handy for straining pasta, removing vegetables from a pot of broth, and turning Homemade Potato Chips (page 43) as they fry. A slotted spoon is simply a metal spoon that is perforated. A frying spider is like a skimmer with a mesh net attached.

### Squeeze Bottles

You put all that time and effort into making the food, so finish it with precision, like a pro. Using a squeeze bottle to dress a plate (see page 108) really finishes the look.

### Stand Mixer

A stand mixer makes kneading bread dough a snap. It's also convenient for mixing cakes and cookies and for whipping egg whites and heavy cream. A hand mixer and a large bowl work for the latter in a pinch.

### Tart Pans

Mini tart pans come in handy for all sorts of preparations, and are essential for Individual Apple Tarte Tatins (page 176).

### Printer

Last but not least is an item you might not think of as part of a culinary arsenal. The printer for your home computer is a handy design and presentation tool. Use it to print custom labels for mini pizza boxes (see page 58), cones for holding French fries (see page 153), soda bottle labels (see page 246), and all manner of personalization that will delight and surprise your guests.

# PASSED

—

*Hors d'Oeuvres,
Savory and Sweet*

**I've become famous for miniaturized versions of favorite comfort foods and hors d'oeuvres with wit and whimsy.** I serve breakfast hors d'oeuvres not only at breakfast events, but also at the end of evening affairs. When the client wants the dancing to last all night, we might pass trays of Breakfast Egg Rolls (page 74) or Mini Fruit Tart Pops (page 83)—it's like a trip to the local diner at three in the morning.

People want that little bit of indulgence, even something rich, if it's just a single bite. Sweet hors d'oeuvres are a great addition to a party. Passing trays of mini dessert items at the end of a cocktail party helps to let people know it's time to go home. The guests may think all the food has been served, but wait—there's more!

My hors d'oeuvres are not complicated, but most are original ideas or twists on a classic item. An hors d'oeuvre tray can be filled with beautiful, classic food that has been served for years and people will enjoy it—but they won't remember it. But when trays bearing our caviar-topped "rings" (see page 49) arrive, guests are surprised and intrigued. Unusual presentations like these become an ice breaker at cocktails and get the guests talking: "Can I actually touch this?" They look at each other to see who will be the first to dare to try a "ring" on their finger. People will remember that for years to come.

I try to create food that makes an emotional connection with the guests— something that goes beyond being attractive and tasty. The food often triggers favorite memories, reminding people of birthday cake from their youth or summer nights spent at an ice cream stand. This food makes people happy and creates an emotional response. Our connection is also achieved through the styling of the food. Often it makes people smile when they see it. When done right, the food concept and styling makes the presentation about much more than food—it becomes a whole experience.

## CAVIAR CAKE

This multitiered stand turns our popular buckwheat blinis with caviar into a "cake." We sometimes use this in place of a birthday or wedding cake. It's an elegant accompaniment to a Champagne toast. (The recipe for the blinis can be found in my book *Bite by Bite*.)

We glue our scallop shells to the serving platter for stability, but you can achieve the same effect at home with these simple ideas:

- Instead of using glue, place a dab of whipped cream cheese on the platter for each shell and set the shell on top.

- Arrange some steamed bitter greens, like Swiss chard or broccoli rabe, on a platter. It will look like seaweed and hold the shells in place.

# SCALLOPS AND PEARLS

I am very fortunate to have summered on Nantucket since high school. One of the things the island is known for is Nantucket Bay scallops, and the beaches along the sound are covered with their beautiful shells. Those shells—and their myriad natural shades of yellow, orange, and red—were the inspiration for this hors d'oeuvre.

Although we use a bay scallop shell as the platform (see the serving tip, opposite, to learn how we made this work), there's a *sea* scallop nestled inside; we cut them down to the proper size for a single bite. At home, you should simply use bay scallops; it's easier and you'll avoid the waste. It is seared, then topped with a dollop of flavorful sauce ravigote and garnished with finely diced cucumbers. Guests can lift the scallop right out of the shell and pop it in their mouth.

*Makes 12*

**For the Ravigote:**

1 shallot, minced

1½ teaspoons white wine vinegar

1 tablespoon plus 1½ teaspoons chopped fresh tarragon

1 cup sour cream

1½ teaspoons finely chopped fresh flat-leaf parsley

1½ teaspoons finely chopped, drained capers

1½ teaspoons finely chopped fresh chives

Coarse salt and freshly ground black pepper

**For the Garnish:**

½ medium cucumber

**For the Scallops:**

12 fresh bay scallops

1 tablespoon grapeseed or other mild vegetable oil

Coarse salt

12 whole sea scallop shells, glued two-thirds open at the hinge, for serving (see opposite)

## SAUCE

In a small saucepan over medium heat, cook the shallot, vinegar, and the 1 tablespoon tarragon until the shallot is soft but not browned, about 3 minutes. Remove the pan from the heat and let cool for about 10 minutes. Add the sour cream, parsley, capers, and chives and mix well. Add salt and pepper to taste. You will have 1 cup of sauce; set aside or cover and refrigerate up to one day ahead until ready to use.

## GARNISH

Peel the cucumber, keeping a small amount of the flesh with the skin. Finely chop the cucumber peels into precise 1/16-inch squares (see Notes). Set aside. Reserve the peeled cucumber for another use.

## SCALLOPS

If necessary, trim the scallops to 1¼-inches wide with a cookie cutter. Heat the oil in a sauté pan over high heat. Lightly salt the scallops and sear on one side until deep golden brown, about 1 minute. Place the scallops, seared side up, on a baking sheet. You can wrap the scallops in plastic and refrigerate them for up to 8 hours before continuing.

When ready to finish the dish, preheat the oven to 350°F.

Warm the scallops for 3 to 5 minutes before assembling the dish.

## ASSEMBLE

Set the 12 scallop shells on a serving platter. Place a warm scallop in the base of the open shell, top with a small dot of sauce ravigote, and garnish with the cucumber. Serve immediately.

## NOTES

If you can't find bay scallops still in the shell at your local fishmonger, you can get the shells online. We use Noble Pectin scallop shells that are 2 to 2½ inches wide.

We used molecular cucumber pearls, but for the home chef, diced cucumber is a good substitute. The easiest way to achieve a small, uniform cut is to stack a few strips of peel and trim them to uniform rectangles. Slice each piece into 1/16-inch-wide sticks; then chop the sticks into 1/16-inch squares.

# WASABI MACARONS WITH SMOKED SALMON

Macarons have always been beloved in New York City, but when the famous Paris bakery Ladurée opened a shop on Madison Avenue, people went crazy for them. I like to take a popular food like this and serve it with a twist. I wanted to do a savory macaron, but we were having a bit of trouble making it work: very few savory flavors pair well with the sugar required in the macaron dough. When our pastry chef added wasabi powder, I knew we had a hit. The wasabi lends a nice color and flavor to the macaron, and it pairs beautifully with the salmon. And people love it because it's a favorite food seen in a new way.

*Makes 25*

### For the Macarons:

1¼ cups sifted confectioners' sugar

½ cup almond flour

Pinch of coarse salt

1 tablespoon wasabi powder

¼ cup egg whites (about 2 large)

2¼ teaspoons granulated sugar

1 drop green liquid food coloring

½ cup finely chopped smoked salmon

25 small dill sprigs

### MACARONS

Line a baking sheet with parchment paper or a Silpat sheet.

Sift the confectioners' sugar, almond flour, salt, and wasabi powder into a medium bowl.

With a hand mixer or egg beater, whip the egg whites and granulated sugar to stiff peaks. Add the food coloring, mixing just to combine. Fold the whipped whites into the dry ingredients and transfer the mixture to a pastry bag fitted with a #804 (³⁄₈-inch) round tip.

Pipe 50 flat 1-inch circles onto the prepared baking sheet. With a damp fingertip, carefully flatten the tops. Holding the baking sheet about 2 inches above the counter, gently drop it onto the counter once or twice to remove any large air pockets. Let sit at room temperature until the surface is dry to the touch. This will take anywhere from 15 minutes to 1 hour, depending on the humidity.

Meanwhile, preheat the oven to 350°F.

Bake the macarons for 12 to 15 minutes, until firm and very lightly colored. Let cool completely, about 10 minutes, and then gently remove from the parchment and set aside.

### ASSEMBLE

To assemble the macarons, set 25 of the macaron rounds on a work surface, flat side up. Divide the salmon evenly among them, making sure the surface of the macaron is covered. Sandwich with the remaining macaron halves.

Attach a small dill sprig to one side of each sandwich by touching the back of the sprig very lightly with water before laying it on top.

# LOBSTER CONES

One of my original hors d'oeuvre ideas was the mini lobster roll, and since it's now become a staple at parties everywhere, I began looking for a new way to serve it. This is a toasted bread cone with a little round scoop of lobster inside. It's delicious, and I particularly like that it's less bready than the roll.

*Makes 12*

### For the Bread Cones:

6 slices very thinly sliced, densely textured white bread, such as Pepperidge Farm Very Thin White Bread (see Note)

12 or 24 large (#801) cake-decorating tips

### For the Lobster Salad:

2 ounces cooked lobster meat, diced

1 teaspoon mayonnaise

Coarse salt

Chopped fresh chives, for garnish

Fresh parsley microgreens, for garnishing the outside of the cones (optional)

Honey (optional)

## BREAD CONES

Preheat the oven to 350°F.

Trim the crusts from the bread. With a rolling pin or your hands, press each slice of bread flat so that it becomes dense and doughy. Cut each slice in half diagonally into 2 triangles.

Roll each bread triangle around a decorating tip with the narrow end of the tip placed at the point at the triangle. Press to seal the overlapping edges and insert the bread-wrapped tip inside another tip to hold it in place. (If you are using 12 tips, work in two batches.)

Lay the cones on a baking sheet and bake for 2 to 3 minutes, until the cones are light golden brown. Let cool and then gently slide the cones off the cake-decorating tips. (The bread cones can be made a day ahead to this point. Store in an airtight container at room temperature overnight.)

## LOBSTER SALAD

In a small bowl, toss together the lobster, mayonnaise, and salt. Do not overwork the salad; mix just to combine. (The lobster salad can be made up to 6 hours ahead and refrigerated until serving.)

## SERVE

Carefully spoon a small amount of the lobster salad into each bread cone. Garnish the salad with chopped chives and, if you like, sprinkle the cones with parsley. (First brush the cones with dots of honey to hold the parsley in place.)

### NOTE

We make all of our breads in-house, but Pepperidge Farm Very Thin White Bread will work well here. It has a fine, dense, even texture and is very thin yet sturdy enough to be rolled flat and manipulated. If you can't find it at your local grocery, you can order it online.

# MINI "LOBSTER" BAKE

Having spent all my summers on the water, I find the clambake one of the most all-American staples of summer. This mini version is a substantial hors d'oeuvre that could also serve as a first course. A small metal sand pail holds one whole cooked crayfish and two cooked, shelled crayfish tails, a salt-baked baby potato, and fresh baby corn. For easier eating, throw in a wooden fork. Check with your local fishmonger for cooked whole crayfish and tails; you can also order both online (see Sources, page 251). Fresh baby corn is appearing more frequently at farmer's markets, but if you can't get it locally, just use the canned variety.

*Serves 8*

2 cups coarse salt

8 peewee or marble potatoes

8 ears baby corn

2 cups clam broth

8 cooked whole large crayfish

16 cooked crayfish tails, shells removed

1 bunch of fresh flat-leaf parsley, for serving

16 lemon wedges, for serving

Preheat the oven to 350°F.

Spread out the salt to fill a half-sheet pan. Set the potatoes about 1 inch apart on the salt bed, pushing them down a bit into the salt. Bake until tender, about 20 minutes.

If using fresh baby corn, place the ears in a steamer over boiling water and cook until tender, 3 to 5 minutes. Lay the baby corn across a heated grill pan just long enough to color with grill marks, 3 to 5 minutes.

In a large pot over medium-low heat, heat the clam broth (do not bring to a boil). Add the whole crayfish and the tails and heat just until warmed through, 3 to 5 minutes. Reserve ¼ cup of the cooking broth and drain the crayfish.

To serve, line the bottoms of the pails with parsley sprigs and arrange 1 whole crayfish, 2 tails, 1 potato, 1 baby corn, and 2 lemon wedges in each pail. Drizzle with the reserved hot broth.

**FOR A BIGGER BOARD** Ideally, we like our hors d'oeuvres to be single bites so that if a guest has a drink in one hand, there's no worry about dropping something on the carpet or on their clothes. But this dish is a great example of a starter that could be made a little bigger for a party at home. You'll simply need to serve it on a small plate.

# MINI CHARCUTERIE BOARD

Charcuterie has become very popular—it seems that everyone loves a good selection of preserved meats. We often do a large charcuterie station at events, but this is another example of taking one of our favorite foods and making it mini.

A lot of the fun in this hors d'oeuvre is how the execution plays on the name—it's whimsical and a bit tongue in cheek. If the server says, "I have prosciutto and Fontina cheese," the response is "Okay, great." But if the server says, "I have a charcuterie board," people look a little closer and then they get the joke.

The toast base is cut into the shape of a classic handled cutting board. We used our 3D printer (see page 64 for more on this) to create the custom cutter, but you can easily cut the bread into a square or rectangle to similar effect. The shaped bread is toasted and topped—it's a whole charcuterie board in one bite.

*Makes 1 dozen*

---

6 slices very thinly sliced, densely textured wheat bread, such as Pepperidge Farm Very Thin Wheat Bread (see page 23)

12 ½-inch-square pieces of roasted red pepper

12 1 × ½-inch pieces of Fontina cheese

12 small strips of a preserved meat of your choice (see Note)

1 teaspoon grainy mustard

3 cornichons, quartered lengthwise

12 small chervil sprigs, for garnish

Preheat the oven to 350°F. Line a baking sheet with parchment paper.

Cut 2 cutting board shapes from each slice of bread and place on the prepared baking sheet. Toast until crunchy, 3 to 5 minutes. Set aside to cool slightly.

Place a square of red pepper in the center of each toast. Place the Fontina cheese on top of the pepper and then add a slice of meat. Top with a dot of mustard, the cornichon quarter, and a sprig of chervil for garnish.

---

### NOTE

We use bresaola (dried beef), but soppressata, salami, and prosciutto will all work well.

## MEAT CARVING STATION

When 8 Spruce Street, the spectacular seventy-six-story skyscraper designed by architect Frank Gehry, was completed, it was the tallest residential building in the Western Hemisphere. The building's developers, Forest City Ratner, asked us to cater a birthday party for their star architect, to be held in the building's penthouse.

The affair was to be a cocktail party, but people might be staying later, so we had to plan for more substantial food. I immediately thought of doing a carving station.

A carving station is a very traditional idea and not something that we did often. But the building's interior features organic forms and uses lots of Douglas fir, one of the architect's favorite woods. I had a vision of laying a matching beam of wood the length of the serving table and setting meat above the beam on spikes. This wasn't the meat to be carved, but rather, it would serve as a magnificent version of a butcher case. This was right around the time that the food media was discovering artisanal butchers like they were the new rock stars.

As the picture shows, we adapt this design to the setting using the same beam display, but in different palettes. This one is for a formal engagement dinner. The meat is the star—and it's one of my favorite designs because it really highlights the food. In fact, the food *is* the display. The carving takes place behind it, out of sight. The cuts are small, and guests can choose to make a sandwich or simply have the meat on a small plate.

We make all the meats in-house, except the pastrami, which is purchased from a great New York deli. We make brisket and corned beef—the serving area is like a classic Jewish deli, but done in an updated way.

# MINI REUBEN PRETZEL SANDWICH

We're always trying to come up with ways to elevate our sandwiches—especially our Reubens, because our Reuben sandwiches are *delicious*. We had been serving them on a mini braided loaf of challah, but I always want to up the ante—especially for guests who have been to our parties before. So now we make our Reubens with our mini pretzels as the rolls. They're super delicious and one of our most popular new items.

*Makes 20*

### For the Pretzels:

1 tablespoon active dry yeast

2 tablespoons light brown sugar

1 cup warm (110°F) water

6 tablespoons (¾ stick) unsalted butter, melted

3 cups all-purpose flour, plus more for kneading

2 teaspoons coarse salt

Olive oil, for greasing the bowl

¼ cup baking soda

1 large egg beaten with 1 tablespoon water

Coarse sea salt, for sprinkling

### For the Filling:

4-ounce block of Gruyère cheese

4 ounces corned beef

¼ cup Russian Dressing (recipe follows)

½ cup chopped sauerkraut, very well drained

### NOTE

For a round roll, after the first rise, portion the dough into 1-ounce balls. Slightly flatten each ball and use kitchen shears to snip an X in the top.

## PRETZELS

In a large bowl, dissolve the yeast and brown sugar in the warm water and set aside until foamy, about 10 minutes. Add 2 tablespoons of the melted butter, the flour, and the 2 teaspoons salt and mix to incorporate the ingredients. Turn the mixture out onto a lightly floured work surface and knead until it forms a ball, 2 to 3 minutes. Grease a large bowl with olive oil, place the dough ball in the bowl, and turn it to coat with oil. Cover with plastic wrap and let rise in a warm spot until the dough has doubled in size, about 1 hour.

Punch down the dough and portion into 1-ounce balls (you should have 20). Roll into ropes, then twist into pretzel shapes. (Alternatively, shape into rolls; see Note.) Cover the pretzels with a clean kitchen towel and let rise until puffy, about 20 minutes.

Preheat the oven to 450°F. Line a baking sheet with parchment paper.

In a large pot over high heat, bring 6 cups water and the baking soda to a simmer. Working in batches, carefully drop the pretzels (or rolls) in the water and simmer for 15 to 30 seconds, or until they float. Remove from the water with a slotted spoon and place on the prepared sheet. Brush lightly with the egg wash and sprinkle generously with salt.

Bake for 1 to 2 minutes, or until just beginning to color. Brush quickly with some of the remaining melted butter and return to the oven to bake until golden brown, about 10 minutes. Remove and brush once more with butter after baking. Reduce the oven temperature to 350°F. Remove the pretzels and set aside to cool, about 20 minutes. Reline the baking sheet with fresh parchment.

## FILLING

Meanwhile, slice the Gruyère and the corned beef into 40 squares each to fit the pretzels and set aside.

When the pretzels have cooled, split them in half. Spread each half with Russian dressing and assemble into sandwiches with 2 slices of cheese, 2 slices of corned beef, and a pinch of sauerkraut.

Place them on the prepared baking sheet and warm in the oven just long enough to heat through and melt the cheese, 2 to 3 minutes.

# Russian Dressing

*Makes about 1½ cups*

---

1 cup good-quality mayonnaise or eggless mayonnaise substitute

½ cup ketchup

3 tablespoons sweet pickle relish

In a small bowl, combine the mayonnaise, ketchup, and relish and stir to blend. Refrigerate until ready to use.

# Kosher Catering

With a name like Callahan, I clearly am not Jewish, but I have become one of the most popular kosher caterers in New York. I started a glatt kosher (meaning that we follow the strictest kosher dietary laws under the supervision of rabbis) division in 2006 for two reasons.

The first was a business reason. As a caterer, I work with vendors who can work at many different types of venues. Planners, florists, bands, and photographers in different sectors of the industry can work events at country clubs and hotels, but I can't—these places do their own food. However, their kitchens don't handle kosher food preparation—but I can, and it has expanded my venue base enormously. We've now catered in the Waldorf Astoria and all sorts of private clubs and venues all over the country.

The second reason I started this division was the challenge. People always said that glatt kosher food couldn't taste good and I thought, "Well, that can't be." You can't use foie gras, caviar, obviously shellfish and pork, and you can't use the combination of dairy and meat, so there are limitations, but in my mind that doesn't prevent one from making great food and serving it stylishly. Glatt kosher meat is very good meat, and I wanted to show that it can be delicious.

We started very organically, adding to the business mostly by word of mouth. We were fortunate to get hired for a large and prestigious event when we first started to offer glatt kosher menus, and that really helped us a lot. Now we do all sorts of distinguished charity galas and annual fundraisers as well as private events like weddings and bar and bat mitzvahs. We're pleased and honored to bring our level of style and food to these celebrations—and people always tell us that they just can't believe it's kosher.

Mazel Tov!

**KIDS TO-GO BOXES** I've learned over the years that kids don't want to sit still at parties—they want to be up and around, having fun, and eat on the fly. So I developed what I call "to-go" boxes, with an entire mini-meal that they can carry with them. This one has chicken nuggets, a California roll, Caesar salad, fries, and a mini burger—all the kids' favorite items. We then slide it into a parchment sleeve with a graphic sticker to hold it in place. For a dramatic entrance, we sometimes stack the boxes on long boards, which are carried out between two waiters, or make a very large stack of the boxes on a bar.

**WALKING PAELLA PAN** This is one of our more unusual roaming services—paella served in oversize paella pans, fitted with straps so they can be easily carried. This is a classic paella with shrimp, mussels, cockles, and chorizo. For catering, we put this together differently than you would if making it at home. So that we can execute quickly at the event, we make the saffron rice and sauté the shrimp ahead of time. At the event, we steam the mussels and cockles and warm everything separately. Once everything is hot, we mix it all together and serve. Adam, our co-executive chef, came up with the "walking paella pan" for his own wedding, which we catered.

**ROAMING RAW BAR** This idea was created for a wedding in Maine, where we were told there wasn't room for a stationary raw bar. So I said, "We will bring the raw bar to you." This is a traveling version of our raw bar. Waiters roam among the guests—usually during the cocktail hour—with a complete selection of seafood and the accompanying sauces. This is often more convenient for guests, as they don't have to break off conversation to move to the raw bar location. We also use these roaming concession boxes for sushi, caviar and vodka, candy, and more. We create them in natural wood, white, and also covered with graphics.

Kumamoto

Hammersly Inlet

Wiley Point

Katama Bay

# MINI MEATBALL SUBS

A meatball sub is the classic example of something that, at full size, could never be done at a party. It's traditionally a very heavy meal, but if you shrink it way, way down—we shrink it to about an inch and a half—it might be called adorable and cute and make the guys happy as well. People enjoy sub shop fare in the smaller scale. We shave a little bit of Parmesan over the top and add a baby basil sprig (picking tiny leaves from the very center of the basil stem).

*Makes about 30*

**For the Buns (see Notes):**

¾ cup warm (110°F) water

1 teaspoon active dry yeast

1¾ teaspoons sugar

½ cup nonfat dry milk powder

2 large eggs

2 cups bread flour, plus more for kneading

¾ teaspoon coarse salt

4 tablespoons (½ stick) unsalted butter, room temperature, cut into small pieces

1 teaspoon extra-virgin olive oil

2 quarts Marinara Sauce (page 55; substituting 1 small bunch of basil for the oregano)

**For the Meatballs:**

2 teaspoons extra-virgin olive oil

4 garlic cloves, minced

1 pound ground beef (20 percent fat)

1 cup bread crumbs

2 large eggs

1 cup grated Parmesan cheese

½ cup chopped fresh flat-leaf parsley

¼ cup heavy cream

1 tablespoon coarse salt

1 teaspoon freshly ground black pepper

½ cup shaved Parmesan cheese, for garnish

Baby basil sprigs, for garnish

*(recipe continues)*

## BUNS

In the bowl of a stand mixer, whisk together ¼ cup of the warm water, the yeast, and ¼ teaspoon of the sugar. Cover with plastic wrap and set aside until foamy, about 5 minutes.

Uncover and add the remaining ½ cup warm water, the remaining 1½ teaspoons sugar, the powdered milk, 1 egg, and 1 cup of the bread flour. Sprinkle the salt over the flour and beat with the paddle attachment on low speed until the mixture is moistened, 1 to 2 minutes. Increase the speed to medium-high and beat the dough until smooth, about 10 minutes.

Stop the mixer and switch to the bread hook attachment. Add ¼ cup of the remaining bread flour and mix on low speed until most of the flour is absorbed. Add a few butter cubes and beat until incorporated. Then add another ¼ cup of the flour. Continue to alternate adding flour and butter until they're both completely incorporated and the dough cleans the side of the bowl during mixing, about 7 minutes (add 2 to 3 more tablespoons flour if needed).

Turn the dough out onto a lightly floured work surface and knead until it forms a ball, 2 to 3 minutes. Grease a large bowl with the olive oil, place the dough ball in the bowl, and turn it to coat with oil. Cover with plastic wrap and set aside until the dough has doubled in size, about 1½ hours.

Punch down the dough, turn it out onto a lightly floured work surface, and divide it in half. Roll each piece into a log 12 inches long and 1 inch wide. Cut each log into 18 pieces. Roll each piece into an oval and slightly flatten it. Place the pieces on a parchment-paper-lined baking sheet, leaving 2 inches between them. Cover with plastic wrap and let the dough rise in a warm, draft-free spot until the loaves are about ½ inch high, 12 to 15 minutes.

Meanwhile, preheat the oven to 350°F.

In a small bowl, whisk the remaining egg with 2 tablespoons water. Lightly dab the top of each dough ball with the egg wash. Bake until the buns are golden brown, about 10 minutes, rotating the baking sheet halfway through. Remove from the oven and set aside to cool completely, about 20 minutes.

## MEATBALLS

In a 5- or 6-quart pot, bring the marinara sauce to a slow simmer over low heat.

Heat the oil in a small sauté pan over medium heat. Add the garlic and sauté until just soft, but not browned. In a large bowl, combine the sautéed garlic, ground beef, bread crumbs, eggs, Parmesan, parsley, cream, salt, and pepper and mix thoroughly with clean hands. Shape the meat into 1-inch balls (we use a #100 disher). You'll want to fit at least 2 meatballs into each mini sub.

Add the meatballs to the sauce and simmer until cooked through, about 15 minutes.

## SERVE

Use a serrated knife to slice each bun at a 45-degree angle, starting at the top right corner and slicing three-quarters of the way through the roll. Place 2 meatballs in each roll, dust with shaved Parmesan, and top with a sprig of basil. Serve warm.

---

*NOTES*

Substitute your favorite recipe for the rolls if you prefer. Or, if you're short on time, buy King's Hawaiian dinner rolls and cut them down to 2½ inches in length.

You will have extra marinara sauce after assembling the heroes; freeze it for another use.

# How Many Courses?

We do dinners with four (or more) courses with some regularity. These are usually for clients who consider themselves foodies and who want the emphasis on the dinner served in multiple courses. That adds a whole different set of criteria. First, you have to be sure the courses aren't too filling. We've all been taught to eat what's in front of us and even if you have a menu card advising guests of how much food is ahead, people will eat what's on their plate. Your job as a caterer is to make sure that you have enough food, but—just as important—that the portions aren't too big.

The majority of the dinner parties we do have two savory courses before dessert, so clients typically want something a little bit filling as the first course. For that reason we don't often do a soup. But especially when entertaining at home during the winter months, when an entrée may be heartier, soup makes a great first course. And when we serve multiple courses, a soup is a wonderful thing.

Risotto is a very popular component of a multiple-course meal. A pasta course is another—we like to do ravioli, either in wonton wrappers, so they're steamed, or open-faced, which highlights the ingredients and lets people choose how much pasta they want to eat. And we quite often serve a cheese course at the end.

GRAVLAX

HALIBUT

SALMON

TUNA

PERFECT PRESENTATION

**FISH CARVING STATION**  I cater a number of events where the food must be kosher (see Kosher Catering, page 32). Because meat and dairy products cannot be mixed, clients choose a menu based on one or the other. One large celebration had a dairy menu, but we wanted it to be hearty, so I suggested a fish carving station, which was a big hit. We mimicked the idea of the meat carving station, with a central beam that displayed all the fish available. The guests could help themselves to the many garnishes and accompaniments.

# HOMEMADE POTATO CHIPS

The whole idea for this hors d'oeuvre is high/low. We first made them for a very fancy wedding. The couple wanted something interesting to be served before the ceremony—a little snack accompanied by Pellegrino or Champagne. Service was to be in a very ornate marble foyer. The juxtaposition of simple potato chips in paper cones against a beautiful silver tray is what made it a great addition to a party. It's a little campy serving potato chips on a silver-tone tray. We printed the monogrammed cones, which were lined with parchment paper. The tray was highly polished stainless steel; we drilled holes to hold the cones. You also can find many different platforms to hold cones online (see Sources).

*Makes 18 to 20 cones of 8 to 10 chips*

Vegetable oil, for frying     Fine sea salt

4 Idaho potatoes, scrubbed but not peeled

Line a baking sheet with 2 or 3 layers of paper towels.

Pour about 2 inches of oil into a deep 10- or 12-inch sauté pan and heat to 300°F. (If you don't have a thermometer, drop in a potato slice as a test. If the oil begins to bubble, it's ready.)

Carefully use a mandoline (see Note) to slice 1 potato very thinly. Fry the slices until crisp and golden, about 3 minutes.

Use a spider or slotted spoon to lay the chips in a single layer on the lined baking sheet. Sprinkle immediately with fine sea salt.

Repeat with the remaining potatoes, making sure the oil comes up to temperature before starting each batch. Store the chips in an airtight container until ready to serve.

---

*NOTE*

A mandoline will give you very thin, uniform slices, but if you don't have one, you can use a vegetable peeler.

# BACON AND MAKER'S MARK

Bacon is such a delicious food with a fanatical following that you don't need to do anything to it—we like serving it all by itself. We started off by serving just a little crispy square of bacon that stands up vertically on the tray. People were always surprised: "What's this?" they'd ask. And we'd simply reply, "It's bacon!" I've been told by the most illustrious party planners that this is their favorite hors d'oeuvre.

We started pairing bacon with bourbon at a wedding for a couple with Southern connections. We bought mini bottles of Maker's Mark bourbon (see Sources, page 251)—they have an iconic red wax seal on the cap, which is why I like their look. We drilled through the wax and the metal cap with a drill bit that is a bit wider than the straw, emptied out the bourbon—which was then mixed with apple cider and sparkling water and funneled back into the bottle. (You could simply remove the cap and mix your favorite bourbon cocktail.)

Finally, we inserted a matching red straw, and served the bacon squares alongside.

*Makes 12 to 16*
*(depending on the size of your bacon)*

Preheat the oven to 350°F.

Line a quarter-sheet pan with parchment. Lay the bacon strips on top of the parchment and cover with a second sheet of parchment. Set a second quarter-sheet pan on top to keep the bacon flat.

Bake until the bacon is almost cooked but still flexible, 10 to 15 minutes. Remove from the oven and discard the top sheet of parchment. With a sharp knife, cut the bacon into 2-inch pieces.

Return the bacon to the oven and cook, uncovered, to desired doneness, another 5 minutes or so. Transfer to a paper-towel-lined plate to drain.

Use a power drill to drill a hole in the top of each bottle. Arrange the mini bottles of bourbon on a serving tray and insert mini red drinking straws (see Note). Lean the bacon square against the bottle.

---

### NOTE

As an alternative, you can serve the bourbon—or your favorite bourbon cocktail—in a shot glass, using the same red straws; simply lean the bacon against the glass instead of the bottle.

---

12 slices thick-cut, applewood-smoked bacon

12 mini bottles Maker's Mark bourbon (see Sources)

## DIM SUM DISPLAY

What does the person most famous for shrinking food do next? We supersize it. Or at least, we supersize the display.

The idea for this display brought dim sum back onto our menu. We love dim sum and it's very popular, but we needed a new way to present it—what could we do to take it to a whole new level? Well, we've miniaturized a Chinese food take-out box; now let's blow it up.

These giant boxes lend themselves to custom graphics that make the display even better. We lay a sheet of acrylic just below the opening and cover that with a nest of fried cellophane noodles or parsley. Then we set the dumplings on top. Like all my displays, it allows us to set the food at different levels, but it's still very easy for guests to serve themselves.

Flat pegboards that our prop team makes in-house are set at either end of the display to hold the chopsticks vertically, while small bowls of dipping sauces and toppings are set at the front, along with lo mein and crispy noodles.

Vegetable Potstickers

# PEKING DUCK STEAMED BUNS

Chef David Chang brought so much attention to steamed buns at his New York restaurant Momofuku (and rightly so—they are amazing) that I thought this would be another great take on a mini version of a very comforting food.

The trick to success here is to make the buns small, but with enough room for the filling without being too doughy. So we roll the dough a bit thinner than we would for a full-size bun. We make this super-delicious bite with two different fillings: here we use purchased Peking duck, but we also do a version with pork belly.

We present these on a bed of baby greens in mini bamboo steamer baskets. The red baskets set against the dark metal tray make a dramatic display, but these could be served on any plate or platter.

You can buy frozen Chinese buns (*bao*) in most Asian markets, but they are large. Thaw the dough, cut it to the desired size, and steam as described at right.

*Makes 36*

### For the Steamed Buns:

1 tablespoon active dry yeast

3 tablespoons sugar

1 cup warm milk

1 tablespoon vegetable oil, plus more for the bowl and brushing

2 cups cake flour

1 cup all-purpose flour, plus more for dusting

½ teaspoon coarse salt

### For the Filling:

¾ cup hoisin sauce

1½ cup julienned roast duck meat (from a store-bought Peking duck), cut to the length of the buns

¾ cup thinly sliced crispy roast duck skin

3 scallions, green part only, sliced, for garnish

## BUNS

In the bowl of a stand mixer fitted with the paddle attachment, combine the yeast, sugar, and milk. Let sit until the mixture is foamy, about 10 minutes.

Add the oil, cake and all-purpose flours, and salt to the milk and beat on medium speed until a smooth, elastic dough is formed. Grease a large bowl with vegetable oil, place the dough in the bowl, turn it to coat with oil, and cover with plastic wrap. Let rise until doubled in size, about 1 hour.

Turn the dough out onto a floured work surface and roll it ⅛ inch thick. Use a 2-inch oval or round cutter to cut out 36 buns. (If you have only a round cutter, gently tug the rounds into oval shapes if you'd like.) Brush one side of each bun lightly with oil and fold in half crosswise, oiled side in, pressing lightly.

Fill a pot wide enough to snugly hold the bamboo steamer halfway with water and bring to a boil over high heat. Reduce the heat to medium and set a bamboo steamer on top. Working in batches, place the folded buns in the steamer with at least ¾ inch between them and steam for 10 minutes. Remove from the steamer and set aside to cool. At this point, you can freeze the buns for later use. Place them in a single layer on a parchment-lined baking sheet and freeze until firm, then transfer to freezer bags. The buns can be frozen for up to 2 months.

## ASSEMBLE

When you're ready to fill the buns, bring the water under the steamer back up to a boil. Open each bun and place a small bead of hoisin sauce on the bottom half. Fill with 3 or 4 pieces of duck meat. Return the buns to the steamer for about 5 minutes to warm them through.

## SERVE

Top each bun with another dot of hoisin sauce, a slice of crispy skin, and a scallion ring. Serve warm.

**CAVIAR IS FUN, NOT FANCY** I don't use caviar to be hoity-toity—that's not my style. I like flavors that have universal appeal, and for this group of hors d'oeuvres, the taste of the caviar pairs very well with the cracker. Plus the caviar looks great! We use American caviar, which is very reasonably priced (it's paddle fish roe). It's meant to be fun, not fancy.

# CAVIAR RINGS

Darcy Miller has been editor at large and an integral part of *Martha Stewart Weddings* from its beginning and is the author of *Celebrate Everything!* She is one of the greatest talents in the business. She and I have been collaborating on parties for more than fifteen years. This hors d'oeuvre is the result of a brainstorming session we had for Dylan Lauren's engagement party. Dylan, the daughter of Ralph Lauren, is the owner of Dylan's Candy Bar, and Darcy's theme for the engagement party she hosted was jeweled candy.

I've done a lot of parties for Dylan over the years so I really wanted to come up with something new and special. It was Darcy who suggested a ring—and now it's one of the most popular hors d'oeuvres we do for weddings and engagement parties.

We created a tray similar to a jeweler's tray to hold the rings. Our version is made from a slab of acrylic that's drilled with a laser cutter to create a little slit that holds the ring. We torture our chefs with this one. The "ring" has to be the exact right size to fit the notch in the tray. We designed and made the trays in two days in order to have everything ready for Dylan's engagement party. The reaction from the guests made it worth all the effort.

The ring is a combination of two crackers: the round ring and the small square cracker that serves as the "setting" for the caviar jewels. The two crackers are glued together with a dot of cream cheese. Our chefs developed the perfect dough for the cracker: it's just strong enough that it won't break, but still light in texture and taste.

We sometimes pair these with mini glasses of Champagne and pass them right before the cake cutting at a wedding reception.

*Makes 50*

1 cup all-purpose flour, plus more for rolling

¾ teaspoon coarse salt

3 tablespoons cold unsalted butter, cut into ⅛-inch dice

¼ cup finely grated Gruyère cheese

⅓ cup milk

1 tablespoon whipped cream cheese

3 ounces caviar (see tip box, opposite)

Combine the flour, salt, and butter in a food processor and pulse until the mixture resembles coarse meal. Add the cheese and pulse until combined. Add the milk and pulse just until the dough comes together. Wrap the dough in plastic and let rest at room temperature for 20 minutes.

Preheat the oven to 250°F. Line two baking sheets with parchment paper.

Lightly flour your work surface and a rolling pin. Roll the dough ¹⁄₁₆ inch thick. Using a 1¼-inch round cookie cutter, cut 50 circles. Use a ½-inch cutter to remove the center of each circle, making a ring. Gather up and reroll the scraps. Using a ¾-inch square cutter, make 50 tops. (If you have extra dough, refrigerate it for another use or cut the scraps into crackers to bake as a snack.)

Place the ring circles on a lined baking sheet; place the square tops on the second lined baking sheet. Cover the tops (but not the circles) with parchment and another baking sheet. Bake together on racks placed near the center of the oven for 30 minutes. Rotate the pans front to back, uncover the ring tops, and bake for 15 to 30 minutes more, until the crackers are crisp and lightly colored. Let cool completely, about 15 minutes.

To assemble the rings, use the cream cheese as "glue" to fasten the square top to the ring. Place the assembled rings in the display, and then top each square with a generous dot of caviar to represent the gem.

## VARIATIONS ON A CRACKER

The cracker recipe used for the Caviar Rings (page 51) is a favorite—it tastes good and is sturdy enough to be adapted to a number of different shapes. A skull and crossbones drink and hors d'oeuvre pairing (opposite) is a must for Halloween (although the skull motif has become so popular that we serve it year-round). When I saw miniature skull-shaped bottles, I knew we had to do something with them. These bottles look so cool, they could have been designed by the artist Damien Hirst. Naturally, we filled the bottle with a blood-red Pomegranate and Blackberry Martini (page 243) to be sipped through a matching black straw. To accompany it, we went back to our favorite cracker recipe, this time cut into bone shapes that were crossed and then topped with a bit of caviar. Skull and crossbones!

Make the cracker dough as directed for Caviar Rings. Use a 1½-inch bone-shaped cookie cutter to cut out 50 bones. Gather up and reroll the scraps as needed. (If you have extra dough, refrigerate it for another use or cut the scraps into crackers to bake as a snack.) Bake as directed and let cool completely (about 15 minutes). Use a dot of whipped cream cheese to attach two bones together in a cross. Place a generous dollop of caviar on top, where the bones join together. (You'll need 1½ ounces of caviar for the 25 crossed-bone crackers.)

The caviar musical notes (below) were developed for a party celebrating the acquisition of a stylish headphone company by a computer giant. We were asked to provide food that was hip and on point with a musical theme, and these hit the perfect note. The event was on a yacht hosting a music superstar's birthday party.

Make the cracker dough as directed in the recipe for Caviar Rings. Use a 2-inch musical note–shaped cookie cutter for the crackers. Gather up and reroll the scraps as needed. You should have 50 notes. Bake as directed and let cool completely, about 15 minutes. Place a dollop of caviar on the round end of the cracker to simulate a musical note. (You'll need 3 ounces of caviar for the 50 crackers.)

PERFECT PRESENTATION

# A TRIO OF MINI PIZZAS

Mini pizzas have been on catering menus for years, but they were never on mine because I found them too ordinary. But when I thought of making mini pizza boxes, mini pizzas went on my menu, too. Now they entertain guests and the boxes are often personalized to the party.

We customize the box lids: for a wedding it's printed with the couple's names and the date; for a kid's party, with the child's name and birthday. The boxes are glued to the trays and guests simply lift the pizza from the box.

We serve our pizzas with three different toppings: mozzarella with the classic basil and tomato; pepperoni; and a more sophisticated fig, leek, and shallot combination. We originally did round mini pizzas, but now we do mini pizza wedges that give the effect of a delivery pizza. Mini pizzas went on my menu and then the mini boxes went viral.

*Makes 30*

½ teaspoon sugar

1½ teaspoons active dry yeast

⅓ cup warm (110°F) water

1 cup all-purpose flour, plus more for kneading and rolling

¾ teaspoon coarse salt

1½ tablespoons extra-virgin olive oil, plus more for the bowl

In a medium bowl, stir together the sugar and yeast. Stir in the water and set the mixture aside for 10 minutes, until it starts to foam.

Lightly flour a work surface. Stir the flour, salt, and oil into the yeast mixture; then turn the dough out and knead, adding a little more flour as needed, until a soft, smooth dough forms. Place in an oiled bowl, turn once to coat, and cover with plastic wrap. Set aside in a warm spot to rise for 1 hour.

Preheat the oven to 350°F and line a baking sheet with parchment paper.

When the dough has doubled in size, turn it out onto a floured surface and roll it ⅛ inch thick. Prick the surface all over with a fork. With a 1¾-inch cutter, cut the dough into circles. (Alternatively, use a 4-inch round cutter, and then cut each circle into 6 wedges after baking.) Gather up and reroll the scraps, letting the dough rest for a few minutes before rolling and cutting if it's very stretchy.

Lay the dough circles on the prepared baking sheet, cover with a piece of parchment and a second baking sheet, and bake for 5 minutes. Flip the crusts over and bake, uncovered, for 5 to 8 minutes more, until they just begin to color. Let cool completely. (If you baked larger circles, cut each into 6 wedges.) The pizza crusts can be frozen at this point for future use; let them thaw completely before topping.

*(recipe continues)*

# MINI PIZZAS WITH BASIL, TOMATO, AND MOZZARELLA

*Makes 10*

---

10 baked mini pizza crusts (see page 54)

1 tablespoon extra-virgin olive oil

8 ciliegine mozzarella balls (about 1 inch in diameter), thinly sliced

6 red grape tomatoes, thinly sliced

6 yellow grape tomatoes, thinly sliced

10 mini basil leaves, for garnish

Sea salt

Preheat the oven to 400°F.

Place the crusts on a baking sheet and brush them lightly with the olive oil. Add the cheese and tomato slices, alternating them. The toppings should cover the crust surface and overlap slightly. Bake for 3 to 5 minutes, until the cheese is just softened and the pizzas are heated through.

Garnish each pizza with a basil leaf and sprinkle lightly with salt. Serve immediately.

# MINI FIG, LEEK, AND ONION PIZZAS

*Makes 10*

---

10 baked mini pizza crusts (see page 54)

**For the Caramelized Shallots:**

10 pearl shallots

1 tablespoon extra-virgin olive oil

¼ teaspoon coarse salt

Freshly ground black pepper

**For the Leek Circles:**

1 large leek (1½ to 2 inches in diameter), light green part only, sliced into ¼-inch rings

1 teaspoon extra-virgin olive oil

¼ teaspoon coarse salt

¼ cup fig jam

¼ cup goat cheese

¼ cup grated Sottocenere cheese with truffles

10 very small thyme sprigs

Preheat the oven to 350°F.

Make the caramelized shallots: Toss the shallots with the olive oil, salt, and pepper in a small baking dish and bake, stirring occasionally, until caramelized, 25 to 30 minutes.

Make the leek circles: You'll need 10 leek circles. Place the leeks in a separate baking dish. Drizzle with the olive oil and sprinkle with salt. Bake until tender but not colored, about 5 minutes.

Increase the oven to 400°F. Arrange the pizza crusts on a baking sheet and top each with 1 teaspoon of the fig jam. Divide the cheeses evenly among the crusts and top each with 1 shallot and 1 leek circle. Bake until the cheese begins to melt and the pizzas are hot. Top each with a small thyme sprig.

# MINI PEPPERONI PIZZAS

*Makes 10*

---

10 baked mini pizza
  crusts (see page 54)

¼ cup Marinara Sauce
  (see recipe, right)

1 thin slice from a
  small ball of fresh
  mozzarella, cut into
  mini circles (see Note)

5 very thin slices of
  pepperoni, cut into
  mini circles (see Note)

Dried red pepper flakes
  (optional)

Preheat the oven to 400°F.

Arrange the pizza crusts on a baking sheet and
spread with about 1 teaspoon of the marinara
sauce. Top each pizza with 3 or 4 pieces of cheese
and pepperoni.

Bake until the cheese is melted and the pizza is
hot. Sprinkle with red pepper flakes if you like,
and serve immediately.

---

### NOTE
We use round cake-decorating tips to cut the mozzarella
and pepperoni into rounds (a #805, which has a ⁷⁄₁₆-inch
opening, is perfect).

## Marinara Sauce

This recipe makes more sauce
than is needed for the pizzas.
Store the leftover sauce in a
sealed container in the fridge for
up to 1 week or in the freezer for
up to 6 months.

*Makes about 2 quarts*

---

3 tablespoons extra-virgin olive oil

½ onion, finely diced

3 tablespoons minced garlic

3 28-ounce cans crushed tomatoes

1 teaspoon dried oregano

½ teaspoon garlic powder

½ teaspoon onion powder

Coarse salt and freshly ground black
  pepper

Heat the oil in a large saucepan over
medium heat. Add the onion and
garlic and sauté until translucent,
3 to 4 minutes.

Add the tomatoes, bring to a simmer,
then reduce the heat to low. Cook,
stirring occasionally with a long-
handled spoon, until the sauce
has reduced by one-quarter, about
1 hour.

Add the oregano, garlic powder,
onion powder, and salt and
pepper to taste. Simmer, stirring
occasionally, for 20 to 30 minutes
more, until the flavors combine.

## PIZZA STATION

This buffet rose out of our mini pizzas,
which are set in mini boxes and passed
around on trays. We thought, Let's supersize
and decorate a pizza box half open The pizza
looks stylish and original, but is still highly recognizable.

Sometimes we create a pizza station by itself, sometimes
it shares space with other foods on the buffet. This display
repurposes an everyday item in a new way—and it's very
easy to re-create at home. You could go to your local
pizzeria and get some boxes and customize them with a
paper covering with your kid's name on it. Buy the pizza,
too, if you want. The display will have the same impact. We
decorate the boxes in all different ways, from sequin- to
graffiti-covered, depending on the vibe of the occasion.

PERFECT
PRESENTATION

*salumi*

# GRILLED NECTARINES WITH DUCK PROSCIUTTO, PARMESAN, AND BASIL

Although I'm well known for doing miniature comfort foods and whimsical small bites, we do a lot of parties where people just want classic hors d'oeuvres. This is one of those classics. It looks very pretty on the tray and packs a lot of flavor by pairing the sweetness of the nectarine and basil with the saltiness of the duck prosciutto and Parmesan.

*Serves 8*

1 or 2 thin slices of duck prosciutto

1 medium nectarine, cut into 8 wedges

8 small, thin slices of Parmesan cheese

8 ½-inch-long basil leaves

Cut the prosciutto into 8 pieces 1½ inches long.

Trim a thin slice from the round bottom of each nectarine wedge so the slice will stand up on the platter.

Heat a grill or a grill pan over high heat until smoking and grill the nectarine wedges on one side only for about 1 minute (the fruit should have grill marks, but not be cooked).

To assemble, cut a ½-inch-deep slit in the top of each wedge at a 45-degree angle. Layer a piece of prosciutto, a Parmesan shard, and a basil leaf together and slide them into each slit.

SD card

Time left 6 min
Printing:
chickenbone_v2
TUNE          PAUSE

Ultimaker

# MINI CHICKEN WINGS

The press always asks me, "Is there any one thing that you haven't been able to shrink?" In the past, my mind always went to chicken wings. I'm always shrinking some common, everyday, casual American food that everyone loves. Chicken wings are one of those things. And of course wings wouldn't normally be served at a fancy party, which made the problem even more attractive to me—how could I make them so they'd work for any occasion? Along the way we tried to use a quail drumstick, but it was just too boney and too expensive. It dogged me for a long time, but a few years ago, I came up with the answer.

When you order chicken wings, you get half winglets and half drumettes. I realized we had to work with the drumettes because you can't re-create the winglets. (We tried.) We could form the drumette shape from ground chicken, but you have to have the bone. We literally tried everything to figure out a good-looking faux bone, and then we discovered 3D printing (see the sidebar on page 64).

For the meat, we mixed ground chicken (we prefer to use thigh meat for the best flavor) with onions, cheese, and a dose of hot sauce, and then molded it into the shape of the drumette. It's very important not to add the "bone" until the drumettes are out of the oven and cooled down, so that the plastic stays intact. If you're making these at home, I recommend using decorative toothpicks—the wings will taste just as good.

*Makes about 45*

1 pound ground chicken thighs

½ cup minced onion

1¼ cups panko

1 tablespoon garlic powder

⅔ cup grated Parmesan cheese

⅓ cup shredded sharp Cheddar cheese

1½ cups hot pepper sauce (such as Tabasco)

1 tablespoon coarse salt

1 large egg

Vegetable oil, for frying

8 tablespoons (½ stick) unsalted butter, melted

Line a baking sheet with parchment paper.

In a large bowl, combine the chicken, onion, panko, garlic powder, Parmesan and Cheddar cheeses, ½ cup of the hot sauce, the salt, and egg. Mix thoroughly.

Form the meat mixture into small drumstick shapes approximately 2 inches long, placing them on the prepared baking sheet as you go. Place the tray in the freezer for 30 minutes, or until the mixture is firm enough to handle.

Meanwhile, preheat the oven to 350°F. In a deep 10- or 12-inch sauté pan, heat about 3 inches of vegetable oil to 350°F. (If you don't have a deep-frying thermometer, drop in a few panko crumbs. If they sizzle, the oil is hot enough.)

Remove the drumsticks from the freezer and round out the bottom side that's become flattened from sitting on the tray. Carefully drop each piece into the oil and fry a few at a time until golden brown, 3 to 4 minutes. Take care not to crowd the pan and to keep the oil temperature consistent.

Transfer the fried chicken back to the baking sheet and finish cooking in the oven for 4 to 5 minutes.

Meanwhile, in a large bowl, whisk together the remaining 1 cup hot sauce with the melted butter. Working in batches, gently toss the chicken in the mixture to coat. Skewer the narrow end with a frilly toothpick to serve.

# Creating the
# Perfect Faux Bone

After years of trying to develop a mini chicken wing, I finally realized that when we have a deadline, we get things done. So I added it to an event menu and challenged my team to make it work. Then, with the advent of 3D printing technology, I learned that we could make our own bones, which could be inserted into the shaped ground-chicken drumettes after they had baked and cooled.

With the event deadline looming, I visited a 3D printing studio. They gave me a price of almost ten dollars per bone. "Well, *that's* not going to work," I thought, especially since things that are sort of cute might be thought of as favors and sometimes end up in people's pockets.

Looking at the unit cost, and realizing I needed about six hundred bones for one party, I decided to just buy a 3D printer for the company. When I brought it to one of my team members and said, "You're now a 3D printing expert," he looked at me in horror. We couldn't get up to speed on this new technology fast enough, but luckily a group of 3D printing teachers from Brooklyn helped us program the printer and get it up and running—and they came by all weekend to check on us and make sure everything was going right for the party on Saturday.

It's really nice how a community comes together. They didn't know us at all, but they thought what we were trying to create was kind of fun and they understood that we were in a jam. They came to our rescue like superheroes.

We're rolling out chicken wings all the time, and are now on to the next frontier—making edible chicken bones with the help of 3D printers. We use a food 3D printer to produce them and a standard 3D printer to make the molds.

# SPAGHETTI WITH EGGPLANT MEATBALLS

A spaghetti and beef meatball hors d'oeuvre is on the cover of my first book, *Bite By Bite.* When a client asked for a vegetarian version, one of my chefs came up with an eggplant meatball that has become our new favorite—in fact, we like it better than the meat version! Even those who don't care for eggplant love it.

*Makes about 60*

**For the Eggplant Meatballs:**

3 medium eggplants (about 3 pounds), peeled and cut into 1-inch cubes

2½ tablespoons plus 2 teaspoons extra-virgin olive oil

½ teaspoon coarse salt

½ teaspoon freshly ground black pepper

⅔ cup minced shallots

⅓ cup grated Parmesan cheese

1 garlic clove, finely minced

⅓ cup finely chopped fresh flat-leaf parsley

1½ tablespoons finely chopped fresh thyme

¼ cup dried oregano

2 tablespoons white miso

⅔ cup panko, plus more for rolling

Vegetable oil, for frying

**For the Béchamel Sauce:**

4 teaspoons unsalted butter

3 tablespoons diced white onion

4 teaspoons all-purpose flour

1 cup milk

Coarse salt and freshly ground black pepper

**For the Spaghetti:**

4 ounces angel hair pasta

¼ cup Marinara Sauce (page 57; see Note, page 67)

1 tablespoon grated Parmesan cheese

Small basil leaves, for garnish

*(recipe continues)*

## EGGPLANT MEATBALLS

Preheat the oven to 350°F.

In a large bowl, toss the eggplant cubes with the 2½ tablespoons olive oil, the salt, and pepper. Spread the cubes across a baking sheet and roast until tender, about 40 minutes. Set aside to cool.

Heat the 2 teaspoons olive oil in a small skillet over medium heat. Sauté the shallots until translucent but not brown, 2 to 3 minutes. Set aside.

In a food processor, combine the roasted eggplant, Parmesan, garlic, parsley, and thyme and pulse until the eggplant is just chopped. Do not overmix. Gently stir in the shallots, oregano, white miso, and the ⅔ cup panko.

Fill a shallow dish with a layer of panko crumbs. Shape the eggplant mixture into small balls about 1 inch in diameter (we use a #100 disher) and roll them in the panko to coat completely. You should have about 60 balls. Set the balls on a baking sheet and place in the freezer for at least 30 minutes before frying.

In a deep 10- or 12-inch sauté pan over medium-high heat, bring at least 3 inches of vegetable oil to 350°F. Line a baking sheet with paper towels.

Carefully drop a few balls at a time into the hot oil and fry until golden. Using a slotted spoon, transfer the balls to the lined baking sheet to drain.

## BÉCHAMEL SAUCE

In a medium saucepan over medium heat, melt the butter. Add the onion and sauté until translucent, 2 to 3 minutes. Add the flour and whisk well to combine. Cook for 2 to 3 minutes to diminish the flour taste. Add the milk and whisk until thick. Whisk in salt and pepper to taste. Strain the sauce through a fine sieve into a medium bowl; discard the solids.

## SPAGHETTI

Cook the pasta until al dente according to package instructions; drain. Warm the marinara sauce.

## ASSEMBLE

Set the eggplant balls on a baking sheet. Using a two-tined fork (such as a fondue fork), twirl 3 or 4 strands of pasta to make a nest and dip it in the warm béchamel sauce. Slide the pasta nest carefully off the fork onto the top of a meatball.

Keep the assembled hors d'oeuvres warm in a low oven until just before serving. Finish with a dot of warm marinara sauce, a sprinkle of Parmesan, and a small basil leaf.

---

*NOTE*

Feel free to use your favorite marinara sauce for this hors d'oeuvre. If using the recipe on page 57, substitute 1 small bunch of basil for the oregano.

SOTTOCENERE

PARMIGIANO

PECORINO GINEPRO

PROSCIUTTO

**PERFECT PRESENTATION**

**CHEESE AND CHARCUTERIE BUFFET** To top the table, we used chalkboard paper, which is inexpensive and easily found. The rustic platters and wooden boards emphasize the artisanal, handmade quality of the cheeses, charcuterie, and breads. We simply wrote the names of the meats and cheeses right on the chalkboard paper. It's a rustic look that's also very sophisticated. You could do this for bars, dinner buffets, and other setups.

Humboldt Fog

Crémeux de Bourgogne

# STILTON CHEESECAKE WITH BACON-ONION MARMALADE

This is an unexpected hors d'oeuvre—our version of a savory cheesecake. We first made this as a round cake, but it just looked like a little cheese puff, which was not the effect I wanted. So we did it as a wedge, because that's how I think of cheesecake. The bacon and caramelized onion on top provide a great, savory flavor—a rich, jam-like topping that's a little reverse play on the graham-cracker crust that a sweet cheesecake would have. We usually offer this as an hors d'oeuvre, but we also serve it at the end of a meal as a counterpoint to fresh fruit or as part of a cheese plate.

*Makes 32 to 40 small wedges*

**For the Cheesecake:**

Nonstick cooking spray

8 ounces Stilton cheese, at room temperature

1½ packages (12 ounces) cream cheese, at room temperature

2 tablespoons sugar

3 large eggs

⅓ cup all-purpose flour

1 cup sour cream

**For the Marmalade:**

½ pound thick-cut bacon, finely diced

1 sweet onion, finely diced

¼ cup (packed) light brown sugar

1 tablespoon balsamic vinegar

1 teaspoon Dijon mustard

Coarse salt and freshly ground black pepper

## CHEESECAKE

Preheat the oven to 325°F. Lightly coat a pie dish with nonstick cooking spray.

In the bowl of a stand mixer fitted with the paddle attachment, mix the Stilton, cream cheese, and sugar on medium speed. Add the eggs one at a time, scraping down the bowl after each addition. On low speed, gently blend in the flour and then the sour cream.

Pour the mixture into the prepared pie dish and bake just until set and no longer jiggly in the middle, 20 to 30 minutes. Refrigerate until completely cold, about 1 hour.

## MARMALADE

Meanwhile, in a skillet over medium heat, fry the bacon until two-thirds done, about 7 minutes—it should still be chewy and not crisp. Transfer the bacon to paper towels to drain and discard all but 1 tablespoon of the bacon fat from the pan. Over medium heat, sauté the onion in the bacon fat until translucent. Add the brown sugar, vinegar, mustard, and salt and pepper and cook until the mixture reaches a thick, jam-like consistency. Let cool completely.

## ASSEMBLE

Cut the cheesecake into strips about 1½ inches wide; then cut the strips into small triangular wedges. Top each piece of cheesecake with a small spoonful of the marmalade.

# TRUFFLE RISOTTO CAKES

Risotto cakes with truffle slices are a classic hors d'oeuvre—and they're easy. Chill the cooked risotto overnight in the fridge and then just cut out the cakes with a cookie cutter—or simply cut them into 1-inch squares. These also make a great first course in a larger size.

*Makes 80*

---

6 tablespoons (¾ stick) unsalted butter, melted

1 onion, cut into small dice

1 pound Arborio rice

¾ cup plus 2 tablespoons dry white wine

5½ to 6 cups chicken stock

½ cup grated Parmesan cheese

5 tablespoons white truffle oil

1½ tablespoons coarse salt

Vegetable oil, for searing

1 fresh truffle (1 to 2 ounces), thinly sliced

In a 3- or 4-quart pot over medium heat, melt the butter. Add the onion and rice, stir to coat, and sauté until the grains are translucent. Add the white wine and cook, stirring, until the liquid is absorbed.

Add the chicken stock 1 cup at a time and cook, stirring, until all the liquid is absorbed before adding the next measure of stock. When all the chicken stock has been added and is completely absorbed, add the Parmesan, truffle oil, and salt. Stir until thoroughly combined.

Spread the risotto evenly in a 9-inch square pan, making sure the top is completely smooth. Cover with plastic wrap and refrigerate overnight or until completely cold.

With a 1-inch round cutter, cut the firm risotto into circles. Lightly oil a sauté pan, heat over medium heat, and sear the risotto cakes on both sides until golden.

To serve, top each risotto cake with 1 truffle slice.

# BREAKFAST EGG ROLLS

We do a lot of breakfasts for the fashion industry so we're always trying to come up with a new way to do eggs. Enter this breakfast egg roll. Sometimes we add bacon, sometimes bacon and cheese. Who doesn't love a fried breakfast sandwich? Even fashion people will eat something fried if it's small enough—especially if it's stylish, too. But you have to keep it small. And we'd pair these with lighter options.

Note that the egg rolls must be assembled one day ahead and frozen overnight before frying.

*Makes 16*

| | |
|---|---|
| 8 strips of bacon | 16 wonton wrappers |
| 3 tablespoons unsalted butter | 6 ounces sharp Cheddar cheese, thinly sliced |
| 8 large eggs | Chopped fresh chives |
| ¼ cup milk | Vegetable oil, for frying |
| Coarse salt and freshly ground black pepper | |

Lay the bacon in a quarter-sheet pan and place in the center of a cold oven. Heat the oven to 400°F and roast the bacon until completely cooked and crispy, about 20 minutes. Transfer the bacon to a paper-towel-lined plate to drain and cool. Break each bacon strip in half.

Melt the butter over medium heat in a 10-inch skillet. Beat together the eggs, milk, and salt and pepper in a medium bowl and pour into the pan. Let the eggs set and then begin to lift and fold with a spatula to form soft curds. Remove the eggs from the pan when they are just slightly undercooked.

Lay the egg roll wrappers on a work surface and divide the scrambled eggs evenly among them. Top each mound of eggs with 1 slice of cheese and a half strip of bacon; sprinkle with chives. Roll up egg-roll style: fold in each long side and then roll the short edges up from the bottom. Seal the edges with a dab of water.

Place the egg rolls in a lidded container and freeze overnight until solid.

When ready to serve, pour at least 3 inches of vegetable oil into a deep 10- or 12-inch sauté pan. Bring the oil to 350°F over medium heat. (If you don't have a thermometer, drop a small cube of bread into the oil. If the oil begins to bubble, it is ready.) Line a plate with paper towels. Very carefully lower the egg rolls, a few at a time, into the hot oil. Fry until warmed through and golden brown, 2 to 3 minutes. Drain on the lined plate and serve warm.

## WARM BUFFET

I'm always looking for attractive ways to incorporate the nuts and bolts of catering into an attractive display. Back in the day, when serving food that had to remain hot, some used food service heat lamps (and some places still do). Here, we've covered food service bulbs that warm the food with chic shades that double as identification for the dishes below. We do all shapes, colors, and styles of lamp shades, from industrial steel to modern, oversize shades in bright colors or patterns. Above all, this helps solve the long-standing universal puzzle of how to keep food warm on buffets without using chafing dishes.

GRITS

BBQ BEE

# DEVILED SCRAMBLED EGGS

Deviled eggs are one of those iconic retro foods that have really never gone away, but are in need of an update. For breakfast-food hors d'oeuvres we let the egg white become the serving dish for the scrambled yolk. These also welcome different toppings, such as caviar, a dollop of chipotle sour cream, or a tuna sauce for a daytime or evening cocktail hour.

Quail eggs are so beautiful in and of themselves that I often make them part of the display. When we do, the display eggs are always hard-boiled—guests will often pick them up and start to shell them, assuming that they're cooked, and we don't want them to be surprised!

You'll have cooked egg yolks left over from the quail eggs. Chop them into salads or crumble them as a garnish over steamed asparagus or other vegetables.

*Makes 24 egg halves*

### For the Egg Base:

12 quail eggs (see Notes)

### For the Scrambled Eggs:

1 tablespoon crème fraîche, plus more for garnish

½ teaspoon dry mustard

Coarse salt and freshly ground black pepper

2 teaspoons unsalted butter

2 large chicken eggs, beaten

Pinch of paprika

Small celery leaves or fresh herbs, for garnish

## EGG BASE

Prepare an ice water bath and place it next to your work surface. Place the quail eggs in a medium pot and add cold water to cover by 2 inches. Cover the pan and bring to a boil over medium-high heat, swirling the pan a few times as the water heats up (this helps the yolks stay centered in the eggs). As soon as the water comes to a boil, remove the lid and reduce the heat to medium-low. Simmer gently for 5 minutes, then turn off the heat. Use a slotted spoon to transfer the eggs to the ice water bath. Let cool for 5 minutes, then peel the eggs and slice them in half lengthwise. Carefully remove the yolks (see Notes) and reserve for another use. Set the egg white shells aside.

## SCRAMBLED EGGS

In a small bowl, combine the crème fraîche and dry mustard and season with salt and pepper. Melt 1 teaspoon of the butter in a small skillet over low heat and add the beaten eggs. As the eggs begin to set around the edges, add the remaining butter and stir continuously with a rubber spatula. When the eggs are almost cooked through, add the crème fraîche mixture and stir to combine.

## ASSEMBLE

Fill the reserved egg white halves with scrambled eggs and garnish with a pinch of paprika or a dot of crème fraîche and a small celery leaf or herb sprig.

## NOTES

If you can't find quail eggs, medium chicken eggs are a good substitute.

Since quail eggs are small, it can be tricky to remove the hard-boiled yolks. If you like, leave the yolks intact and simply lay the scrambled eggs on top; garnish as described.

# MINI FUNFETTI LAYER CAKE WITH FUNFETTI FROSTING

Many of my clients are very wealthy people who can have anything they want, but guess what they love for dessert? They want cake like Mom made out of a Duncan Hines box! So when we make cakes, people say, "Oh my god, I haven't tasted a cake like this in years!" That's because it's just like the ones *my* mother used to make.

That was the inspiration for this hors d'oeuvre. For years I had talked about wanting to do this kind of cake, and over and over, we tried to do a mini round cake, but it looked too abstract, not like a cake at all. Finally one day I realized it needed to be a wedge. So now we make a midsize layer cake and cut it into bite-size wedges, and it's perfect. Everyone loves cake, but now you have room to try lots of other small desserts.

If it's someone's birthday we'll put little candles on that person's piece or mini sparklers on a few pieces. This dessert can also be made using a favorite cake such as red velvet with cream cheese frosting or yellow cake with vanilla frosting.

*Makes about 48*

### NOTE

Place the assembled cakes in the freezer for at least 20 minutes to facilitate cutting.

**For the Funfetti Cake:**

1 pound (4 sticks) unsalted butter, softened, plus more for the pan

3⅓ cups sugar

3 tablespoons pure vanilla extract

1½ teaspoons coarse salt

4⅓ cups cake flour

2 teaspoons baking powder

12 large egg whites

1½ cups milk, at room temperature

3 cups rainbow sprinkles

**For the Funfetti Buttercream Frosting:**

1 pound (4 sticks) unsalted butter, softened

3 cups confectioners' sugar

2 teaspoons coarse salt

1 tablespoon pure vanilla extract

2 cups rainbow sprinkles

### CAKE

Preheat the oven to 350°F. Lightly grease an 18 × 13-inch baking sheet and line it with parchment.

In a stand mixer fitted with the paddle attachment, cream the butter, sugar, vanilla, and salt on medium speed until fluffy, 6 to 7 minutes. Gradually add the flour and baking powder and mix on medium speed until smooth, about 4 minutes. Add the egg whites and mix on medium speed until well combined, about 4 minutes. Scrape down the sides of the bowl and add the milk, mixing on medium speed until combined, about 2 minutes. Remove the bowl from the mixer and fold in the sprinkles.

Pour the batter into the prepared baking sheet. Bake until the cake is golden brown and starts to pull away from the sides of the pan, about 25 minutes. Let the cake cool in the pan for 10 minutes, then carefully invert the cake over a cooling rack and let cool completely. Peel off the parchment.

### FROSTING

In the clean bowl of a stand mixer fitted with the paddle attachment, cream the butter and sugar at low speed until fluffy, 6 to 7 minutes. Increase the mixer speed to medium and add the salt and vanilla extract. Mix until combined, about 2 minutes.

Cut 4-inch circles of cake from the sheet (you should have 12). Spread 6 circles with buttercream. Top with the remaining 6 circles and frost the tops (but leave the sides bare). Sprinkle the tops with the rainbow sprinkles. When ready to serve, cut each circle into 8 wedges.

# MINI FRUIT TART POPS

Many of us grew up with those popular toaster pastries (the brand name of which we won't mention here), but probably haven't tasted one in years. But a mini version—especially when served on a stick—becomes a fun party addition for adults and kids alike. The challenge with such a small size is to strike a balance between the pastry and the fruit filling. The filling has to be sturdy enough that you can put quite a bit in the pastry without having it leak out the sides. A loose, more liquid filling will not work. The icing and the sugar sprinkles can be color coordinated to fit any party's theme.

*Makes about 20*

### For the Pastry Dough:

1½ cups all-purpose flour, plus more for rolling

1½ tablespoons sugar

½ teaspoon coarse salt

8 tablespoons (1 stick) cold unsalted butter, cut into small dice

3 tablespoons ice water

### For the Fruit Filling:

¼ cup raspberry jam

### For the Frosting:

½ cup confectioners' sugar

Pink sanding sugar

20 mini Popsicle sticks (see Sources, page 251)

**PASTRY DOUGH**

In a large bowl, mix the flour, sugar, and salt. Cut in the butter until the mixture resembles coarse crumbs. Add the ice water and mix until the dough just comes together. Wrap in plastic and chill in the refrigerator for at least 1 hour before using.

Preheat the oven to 350°F. Line a baking sheet with parchment paper or a Silpat.

**ASSEMBLE**

On a floured surface, roll the dough ⅛ inch thick and cut it into forty 2 × 1½-inch rectangles. Transfer half of the rectangles to the prepared baking sheet and lightly wet the edges with water. Spoon ½ teaspoon of the jam in the center of each rectangle, leaving about a ¼-inch border. Cover with a second dough rectangle.

Insert a Popsicle stick in each sandwich and press with the tines of a fork to seal the edges tightly.

Bake for 10 to 15 minutes, until very light golden brown. Let cool completely, about 15 minutes.

**FROSTING**

Meanwhile, make the frosting. In a small bowl, mix the confectioners' sugar with about 1 tablespoon water to make a thick but spreadable glaze.

Glaze the top of each cooled pastry and sprinkle with pink sugar before the glaze dries.

# MINI BANANA SPLITS

Sometimes the idea for a dish starts with the *actual* dish. When we came across these mini sundae dishes, we knew we had to find a way to fill them. They were perfectly proportioned to hold three scoops of ice cream—when a melon baller is the scoop. But you don't necessarily need mini sundae dishes to create the same effect. Use egg cups, vintage coupe Champagne glasses, small berry dishes—any container that's attractive and small will work.

To compose the sundaes, soften three flavors of ice cream just enough to scoop it out with a melon baller or #100 disher and then refreeze until hard. We source the small bananas (they're marketed under different names, such as mini or baby bananas), but sliced bananas work just as well.

This is another hors d'oeuvre that always raises a smile. And although it does involve more than a single bite, who can resist it? It also breaks another of our "rules" by requiring a small spoon and a bowl, but for me, the end result justifies it.

*Makes 8*

8 mini scoops vanilla ice cream (see headnote)

8 mini scoops chocolate ice cream (see headnote)

8 mini scoops strawberry ice cream (see headnote)

16 banana slices

½ cup Chocolate Sauce, homemade (at right) or store-bought

½ cup whipped cream

¼ cup rainbow sprinkles

8 Maraschino cherries

Place one scoop of each flavor of ice cream in a mini sundae dish. Place a banana slice in between scoops. Drizzle each sundae with chocolate sauce and top with whipped cream, sprinkles, and a cherry.

## Chocolate Sauce

*Makes about 2 cups*

1 cup heavy cream

½ cup corn syrup

1 cup sugar

½ teaspoon coarse salt

20 ounces bittersweet chocolate

In a medium, heavy-bottomed saucepan over medium heat, combine 1 cup water with the cream, corn syrup, sugar, and salt and bring to a boil. Place the chocolate in a heatproof mixing bowl and pour the hot liquid over the chocolate. Let sit for 5 minutes, then whisk to emulsify. Store any leftover sauce in a covered container in the fridge for up to 10 days.

## KEEPING IT COOL

We use Cambro coolers to keep food frozen during transport to events and when serving outdoors in hot weather. The cooler holds a series of hotel pans (see page 12): the top pan holds dry ice and the next two trays hold food, which will stay frozen for twenty-four hours. Then we use dry ice pellets in serving containers, which frosts the outside of the ice cream buckets.

We catered an engagement party in Madras, India, that was scheduled for the middle of summer. My suggestion that we do an ice cream buffet was met with an incredulous comment from the client on the other side of the world. "Peter," she said, "you *cannot* have an ice cream buffet in India in the middle of summer!" Knowing we could get dry ice, I told her, "Really, we have a way."

To the amusement of our client and her guests, we served an ice cream buffet in India in the middle of summer—and *everything* stayed frozen.

**WHAT TO DO WITH THE STICK?** Just as we try to keep our hors d'oeuvres to a single bite, we also try to avoid passed food that requires a stick or a utensil. The guests are left with something in their hand and they don't know how to dispose of it—at a loss, a man might tuck the stick into his jacket pocket, but what woman wants to drop it into her evening bag?

For years, caterers positioned a lemon half on a tray so that guests could stick a used skewer or other utensil into it, but I never want my trays littered with discards. Our waiters carry a small box under cocktail napkins that guests drop the stick into.

# FOURTH OF JULY POPS

We make red, white, and blue ice pops for the Fourth of July and serve them all summer long. Mini Popsicle molds and sticks are widely available (see Sources). These treats disappear quickly, so no one has to worry about their melting—on the tray or in the hand. We use custom-made molds that hold 1 tablespoon; use the smallest molds you can find—or make the pops in ice cube trays. These have a patriotic look with fresh strawberry, coconut, and Curaçao liqueur—definitely not the Rocket Pop of days gone by.

*Makes about fifty .67-ounce mini pops or ten 3-ounce pops*

**For the Strawberry Layer:**

½ cup pureed strawberries

2 tablespoons sugar

**For the Coconut Layer:**

7 ounces coconut milk

7 ounces Coco Lopez

½ cup heavy cream

**For the Curaçao Layer:**

½ cup sugar

3 tablespoons Blue Curaçao

1 or 2 drops blue food coloring

### STRAWBERRY LAYER

In a small saucepan over low heat, combine the pureed strawberry and sugar with ¼ cup water. Cook, stirring, until the sugar dissolves. Set aside to cool completely.

### COCONUT LAYER

In a small bowl, mix the coconut milk, Coco Lopez, and heavy cream. Set aside.

### CURAÇAO LAYER

In a saucepan over low heat, combine the sugar, Blue Curaçao, blue food coloring, and 1¼ cups water. Cook, stirring, until the sugar dissolves. Set aside to cool completely.

### ASSEMBLE

Fill mini Popsicle molds a third of the way with the strawberry mixture. Freeze until slushy (about 1 hour) and insert Popsicle sticks; the mixture should be firm enough to hold the stick in place. Return the pops to the freezer until the strawberry layer is completely frozen, about 1 hour more.

Fill the molds two-thirds full with the coconut mixture and let freeze again until completely solid, about 2 hours. Finally, fill with the Curaçao mixture and let freeze, about 2 hours. Unmold and enjoy.

# MINI ICE CREAM SANDWICHES

We are always searching for the next mini item, but this one eluded us for years. Everyone remembers peeling back the paper wrapper to hold onto an ice cream sandwich, so when we make our mini version we place it in a half-bag that's custom printed for the event.

We also make our chocolate wafers more rigid than the store-bought ice cream sandwiches, so the chocolate won't stick to your fingers if you forgo the wrappers. The wafers can be made ahead and frozen for at least one month. Substitute your favorite cookie dough or filling for a variation.

*Makes 25*

---

6 tablespoons (¾ stick) unsalted butter, softened

½ cup granulated sugar

½ cup (lightly packed) dark brown sugar

1 teaspoon pure vanilla extract

2⅓ cups all-purpose flour, plus more for rolling

½ cup cocoa powder

½ teaspoon baking soda

½ teaspoon coarse salt

⅔ cup milk

1½ quarts vanilla ice cream, slightly softened

In the bowl of a stand mixer, combine the butter, granulated sugar, brown sugar, and vanilla. Beat on high until the mixture is fluffy and light in color.

In a large bowl, whisk together the flour, cocoa, baking soda, and salt. Alternate adding the dry ingredients and the milk to the butter mixture, beating between each addition. Mix until just combined. Cover the dough and refrigerate until firm.

Spread the softened ice cream evenly (about ½ inch thick) in a half-sheet pan. Freeze until firm.

Preheat the oven to 350°F. Line two baking sheets with parchment paper or a Silpat.

On a well-floured surface, using a floured rolling pin, roll the dough ⅛ inch thick. (The dough will be sticky, so use plenty of flour on your work surface and rolling pin. If you find it hard to work with, roll the dough between two floured sheets of waxed paper.) Cut into 1 × 1¾-inch rectangles. Transfer the rectangles to the prepared baking sheets, spacing them ½ inch apart, and use the dull end of a skewer to make the traditional dot pattern on each cookie. Bake just until set, 3 to 5 minutes. Transfer the cookies, still on the parchment, to racks to cool completely.

Working quickly, cut the ice cream into 1 × 1¾-inch rectangles with a knife or bench knife. Arrange half of the cookies on a baking sheet, nondotted side up. Place a rectangle of ice cream on each cookie, sandwich with the remaining cookies, dots up, and return to the freezer until ready to serve.

Nutrition Facts
Serving Size 1oz
Servings Per Container 1

Amount Per Serving

Calories                    Calories from Fat
                                    % Daily Value

Total Fat
  Saturated Fat
  Trans Fat
Cholesterol
Sodium
Total Carbohydrate
  Dietary Fiber
  Sugars
Protein

Vitamin

# MINI MILK CARTON MILKSHAKE

This is another remembrance of childhood that always gets a great response. What's a more special memento of school lunches than the single-serving milk carton? We design and print our own mini cartons because people really enjoy the personalized paper accessories that sometimes accompany our hors d'oeuvres. The cartons are the perfect canvas to replicate your invitation or show off your favorite sport, hobby, colors, initials, name, or a significant date. We always leave on the nutrition information box for authenticity!

You can print and assemble your own cartons (see Pinterest or YouTube for options), or serve the milkshakes in shot glasses with a straw. We coordinate the color of the mini straws to the cartons (see Sources, page 251).

This makes a very thick milkshake. If you want a thinner consistency, add more milk.

*Makes six 3-ounce cartons*

5 3-ounce scoops of your favorite flavor ice cream

½ cup milk

Place the ice cream and milk in a blender and blend until completely combined.

---

*NOTE*

For a delicious vegan or dairy-free option, blend the same ratio of your favorite flavor of sorbet or dairy-free ice cream with soy or almond milk.

---

## THE DESSERT HORS D'OEUVRE

Our mini desserts are much more popular than mid- or full-size versions. Guests like the small, one-bite sweets because they can taste a lot of different things rather than committing to one full-size serving. We rarely do large desserts because people will get to try only one item versus sampling lots of options.

We mostly do the mini desserts as a passed hors d'oeuvre toward the end of service. At a cocktail party, even if it's over at 8:00 p.m., the hosts like to have one or two dessert hors d'oeuvres passed because it signals that the event is almost over. It's a subtle way of telling guests it's time to leave.

Other times, after we clear the last savory course, these come out and can be passed around the table or set in the middle. Instead of having your standard petits fours or cookie tray or chocolates, you get something more whimsical.

At some events, people will move from one room to another, say from dinner to a room where there's dancing. We often place a table with dessert hors d'oeuvres between the two spaces—it's a nice signal that the night will last a little longer. And we always get requests to pass items near the dance floor, especially frozen treats.

# CEREAL MILK SOFT SERVE WITH FRUITY PEBBLES CONES

The idea of cereal milk as an ice cream base first came to light from Christina Tosi, the pastry chef at Momofuku. We ramped up the idea by making cereal cones. Use your favorite brand of cereal; we soak Cap'n Crunch. We also make it with Trix and the other high-sugar cereals that if you were lucky, your mom let you have as a kid. It's a great high/low treat.

We make our soft-serve in an Italian ice cream machine, but any home ice cream machine will work.

*Makes 8*

---

1 15-ounce box Cap'n
  Crunch cereal

2 quarts whole milk

1 cup plus 2 tablespoons
  sugar

10 large egg yolks

¼ teaspoon coarse salt

8 mini soft-serve
  cones, store-bought
  or homemade
  (recipe follows)

Pour the cereal into a large bowl and add the milk. Let steep in the refrigerator overnight.

Strain the mixture through a fine-mesh sieve into a 3-quart saucepan, pressing all the milk from the cereal. Discard the cereal. Bring the milk to a boil over medium heat.

In a large bowl, whisk together the sugar and egg yolks until pale in color. Add some of the hot milk to the egg yolk mixture and whisk to combine. Slowly add the tempered yolks and the salt to the milk and cook until the mixture is thick enough to coat the back of a spoon. Strain through a fine-mesh sieve and chill in the freezer container of your ice cream maker for at least 4 hours or overnight.

Churn the mixture until thick according to your ice cream maker manufacturer's instructions. Place in the freezer until just set, but not too hard. Using a star tip, pipe the ice cream into soft-serve shapes on a parchment-lined baking sheet and allow to set in the freezer. Use a spatula to transfer to the cones when ready to serve.

# Fruity Pebbles Cones

*Makes 8*

---

2 tablespoons unsalted butter

4 ounces marshmallows

2 cups Fruity Pebbles cereal

Nonstick cooking spray

In a heavy-bottomed pan, warm the butter and marshmallows over medium heat, stirring occasionally, until melted. Add the cereal and mix until completely coated.

Form the cereal mixture in a single layer around a large (#801) cake-decorating tip that's been coated with nonstick cooking spray. Once molded, remove the cone from the tip, and set aside on a tray to cool, about 20 minutes.

To serve, place the ice cream soft serve shapes on top of the cones and serve immediately.

# PLATED

—

*The Seated Dinner
in Multiple Courses*

**Seated dinners are, for my team, a very different experience than serving a meal in a restaurant.** We are often preparing food for three hundred to five hundred guests who need to be served from the first guest to last of a single dinner course in twelve minutes! So we can't fuss over a plate the way a restaurant chef does. There's never been a set of tweezers in our kitchens—ever.

When I design a dish, I have to visualize exactly how many steps it will take to get the food on the plate. For example, say we're serving 250 people for a dinner. I have to think about how many duplicate plating lines are needed for a warm course. I'll want a minimum of four lines, with each line serving 60 guests. Then I have to figure out how many steps there are on each line. Between garnishing and wiping the plates, if there's a minimum of five steps, I will need 20 people in the kitchen just to be on the lines—plus the people on the ovens, plus the people running food from the ovens to the lines. This turns into an army in the kitchen, and the more complicated the plate, the larger the army.

If we are serving two courses before dessert, we often do a room-temperature first course and then a warm main course to give the kitchen time to recalibrate. For a room-temperature course for a large group of guests, the dish has to be designed to be set up in stages starting up to an hour before it's to be served.

I look for ingredients that won't wilt in that time, or fall, or change in any way while sitting on the plate. I also consider the "waiter factor." Waiters leave the kitchen holding one plate in each hand and they often may have to walk fifty yards or more before they reach the table. They'll often swing their arms a bit as they go, so you want a dish that can pass that stability test. And the dish itself needs to be something that has universal appeal without being too dumbed down.

Many of our techniques are equally helpful in home entertaining, where the goal is to serve your guests a dish that both looks impressive and tastes delicious. It's the same set of guidelines—make it special, but

make it achievable. A great example is a first course that can be set up before your guests arrive.

A two-course dinner can last close to two hours—one very helpful trick we've learned for plating main courses is to have all the vegetable accompaniments for each serving laid out in advance on pieces of parchment. So if you have six people for dinner, you want all of your vegetables precooked—already charred, caramelized, blanched, whatever—and arranged on six pieces of parchment paper set on baking sheets. Then you can pop the baking sheets in the oven for less than ten minutes right before you're ready to serve. Transfer that piece of parchment onto the plate with a spatula and then hold the vegetables in place with the spatula while you slide the parchment from underneath—your vegetables are all beautifully arranged on the plate in one move. That took us only twenty years to figure out!

We've also learned that certain entrées are more forgiving than others—like osso buco and beef short ribs. The longer you cook them, the more tender they become, so you don't have to worry about what time you're serving them.

When planning courses for a large event, the timeline for the evening is paramount. Remember that simple courses take thirty minutes from service to clear: ten minutes to serve, ten minutes to eat, and ten minutes to clear. Main courses take forty minutes: five minutes longer to serve and five minutes longer to eat. We can often beat these times, but it's best to be realistic if you need a concise timeline. So if there is dancing after dinner, or if it's a dinner where people are leaving immediately after, it's good to remember that it takes ten to thirty minutes to get guests to transition from the cocktail area to their dinner seats. A two-course dinner can last two hours—and that's without any speeches or delays.

This chapter includes many of my favorite dishes for seated, multicourse meals. They all meet my criteria for success: they look impressive, taste delicious, and are relatively easy to prepare, with many elements that can be made ahead of time.

# ARTICHOKE MUSHROOM TOWER

This dish has many things going for it, but one of the best is that you can make it up to 45 minutes ahead of serving and it will still look and taste great. Serve it at home and your guests will be amazed—how did you pull that off? Although this is a tower, its structure comes from the artichoke bottom at the base, which is a whole round disk. We stack it with seasonal wild mushrooms, baby greens, frizzled leeks, shards of Parmesan cheese, and a bit of pesto oil. The bok choy flower gives it a nice crown at the top. You can make the artichokes and the mushrooms a day ahead, too. You can also purchase artichoke bottoms that are already cleaned and cooked. If using these, reduce the cooking time to 10 minutes.

*Serves 4*

**For the Artichoke Bottoms:**

3 tablespoons freshly squeezed lemon juice

6 large artichokes

⅓ cup extra-virgin olive oil

1 white onion, thinly sliced

2 carrots, sliced into ¼-inch rounds

3 garlic cloves, crushed

2 tablespoons chopped fresh basil leaves

Coarse salt and freshly ground black pepper

1 cup white wine

2½ cups vegetable broth or water

**For the Sautéed Mushrooms:**

2 tablespoons extra-virgin olive oil

2 cups sliced maitake mushrooms

2 cups sliced trumpet mushrooms

¼ cup minced shallots

Kosher salt and freshly ground black pepper

**For the Sautéed Morels:**

2 teaspoons extra-virgin olive oil

8 whole morel mushrooms, rehydrated if dried

1 tablespoon minced shallots

Coarse salt and freshly ground black pepper

**For the Frizzled Leeks:**

1 cup vegetable oil

2 leeks, white part only, julienned

Coarse salt

½ cup Pesto, store-bought or homemade (page 202)

1 cup shaved Parmesan cheese

2 cups microgreens

1 cup Lemon Dressing (recipe follows)

8 sprigs of edible flowers, for garnish (optional)

## ARTICHOKES

Fill a large bowl with water and add the lemon juice. To clean the artichokes, slice off the stems and about 1 inch of the tops; then remove most of the tough outer leaves. Place in the lemon water until needed.

Warm the olive oil in a large pot over medium heat. Add the onion, carrots, garlic, and basil and season with salt and pepper. Gently cook until the onion is translucent. Add the wine and cook until reduced by three-quarters. Add the artichokes and vegetable broth and simmer until the artichokes are tender, about 35 minutes. Drain the artichokes and let cool, about 15 minutes.

When the artichokes are cool enough to handle, remove the remaining leaves and use a spoon (a grapefruit spoon if you have one) to scrape out the choke; discard it. Set the bottoms aside until you're ready to assemble the dish.

## MUSHROOMS

Preheat the oven to 200°F.

In a deep 12-inch sauté pan, heat the olive oil over medium-high heat until just smoking. Add the

*(recipe continues)*

maitake and trumpet mushrooms. Sauté, stirring, until cooked through and golden brown, 8 to 10 minutes. Add the shallots and cook for 1 minute more. Season with salt and pepper to taste. Keep warm in a 200°F oven until ready to assemble the dish.

### MORELS

In an 8-inch sauté pan, heat the olive oil over medium-high heat until just smoking. Add the morels. Sauté, stirring, until cooked through and golden brown, 8 to 10 minutes. Add the shallot and cook for 1 minute more. Season with salt and pepper to taste. Mix with the maitake and trumpet mushrooms and keep warm in a 200°F oven until ready to assemble the dish.

### LEEKS

Pour the oil into a deep 10- or 12-inch sauté pan and heat to 350°F. (If you don't have a thermometer, drop a small piece of leek into the oil. If the oil bubbles, it's ready.) Carefully drop the julienned leeks into the oil in small batches. Use a spider or slotted spoon to keep them moving in the oil and prevent them from clumping; you want individual straws. When golden brown, about 15 seconds, transfer them to paper towels to drain. Sprinkle with salt immediately.

### ASSEMBLE

Slice all the artichoke bottoms in half horizontally (you will have 12 slices for 4 plates). Place a dot of pesto on each plate and then 1 slice of the artichoke bottom. Top the artichoke bottom with 1 teaspoon pesto and ¼ cup of the sautéed mushrooms topped with a few shards of Parmesan. Top with another slice of artichoke bottom. Lightly dress the microgreens with the lemon dressing. Add ¼ cup of the dressed microgreens and top with a pinch of the frizzled leeks. Place a third slice of artichoke on top and garnish with more dressed microgreens and an edible flower garnish, if using. Decorate the plate with dots of pesto, if you like.

# Lemon Dressing

*Makes about 2½ cups*

2 large shallots, peeled

1¼ cups plus 1 tablespoon extra-virgin olive oil

4 lemons

¼ cup mirin

¼ cup rice wine vinegar

1 teaspoon coarse salt

½ teaspoon freshly ground black pepper

Preheat the oven to 350°F. Place the shallots in a small baking dish and toss the shallots lightly with the tablespoon of olive oil. Roast until soft, about 25 minutes.

Zest 2 of the lemons (you should have 2 tablespoons zest) and set aside. Juice all 4 lemons for ¾ cup lemon juice.

Combine the lemon juice, shallots, mirin, vinegar, salt, and pepper in a blender or food processor. With the motor running, add the remaining oil in a slow, steady stream until incorporated. Add the lemon zest and pour into a glass jar or squeeze bottle.

## *Variation:*

### LOBSTER TOWER

We also do a version of this dish that uses lobster instead of the wild mushrooms. Lobster is a very popular first course and it's especially nice if you have only one main course: there is a surf, then a turf, and then a dessert. And the mushroom version becomes a vegetarian option.

Follow the recipe for the artichoke mushroom tower but replace the mushrooms with steamed lobster. Two whole lobsters will make 4 lobster towers. Replace the first layer of mushrooms with half a tail. Split the tail lengthwise and cut it into pieces while maintaining the shape of the tail put back together so it will fit nicely on the tower. Then replace the mushrooms on the top layer with the meat, left intact, from 1 lobster claw.

**THE SEASONAL PLATE** "Farm to table" is obviously the phrase du jour these days, but it just makes sense. You always want to serve foods that are (a) in season; (b) grown locally; and (c) capture the feeling of superfresh ingredients. People want to know what it is that they're eating just by looking at the dish and its ingredients, so we're always looking to highlight just the ingredients themselves, not what we did to them. We often do this by leaving stems on tomatoes, keeping a little bit of the carrot tops intact, or garnishing a dish with peas still sitting in the pods.

# CAPRESE SALAD

This salad never goes out of style: it just makes people think of summer. We add watermelon to lighten the dish and give another layer of flavor. Sometimes we serve this salad family style, or we serve a family-style charcuterie platter with it. We'll use prosciutto, Serrano ham, beef bresaola, and perhaps duck prosciutto. The platter is a nice addition that pairs well.

*Serves 4*

5 to 6 pounds heirloom tomatoes, preferably in different colors

Sea salt

4 cups ¾-inch cubed watermelon

2 8-ounce balls fresh mozzarella cheese, torn into 1-inch pieces

Extra-virgin olive oil, for drizzling

12 to 16 basil sprigs, for garnish

Basil Oil for the plate (optional; recipe follows)

Cut the tomatoes into 1-inch wedges (you want 24 to 32 wedges) and sprinkle with salt. Arrange 6 to 8 tomato wedges on each plate and tuck 3 to 5 pieces each of the watermelon and mozzarella into the empty spots. Drizzle lightly with olive oil and garnish with basil sprigs. Garnish the plate with a few drops of basil oil for extra visual appeal, if desired.

## Basil Oil

*Makes about 1 cup*

1 cup (packed) fresh basil leaves

⅓ cup vegetable oil

⅓ cup extra-virgin olive oil

Prepare an ice bath and bring a 3-quart pot of water to a boil over high heat. Blanch the basil leaves in the boiling water for 15 seconds; then, using a spider or large slotted spoon, transfer them to the ice bath. Drain and coarsely chop. Place the leaves in a blender or food processor, along with the oils. Puree for 3 to 4 minutes, until the mixture is bright green. Strain through a very fine mesh sieve into a glass or squeeze bottle.

# A TRIO OF EGGS

Everyone loves eggs, and little is required to elevate a simple scrambled egg to an elegant first course like this one. The trick here is to keep the eggs warm and moist, so they're cooked until just set and then spooned into the shells. They'll continue to cook on their way to the table. Each egg has a different topping: caviar, foie gras, and shaved truffle. A bed of salt is built up on the plate to hold the shells in place. We purchase egg shells that have been cleaned and sterilized (see Sources, page 251), choosing a variety of colors and patterns.

*Serves 4*

4 cups flaky sea salt or kosher salt

12 egg shells, in a variety of patterns and colors, cleaned and tops removed to make a cup

4 tablespoons (½ stick) unsalted butter

12 large eggs

½ cup milk

Coarse salt and freshly ground black pepper

2 teaspoons caviar

2 ounces foie gras, sliced, seared on both sides, and cut into small pieces

2 teaspoons shaved truffle

Mound 1 cup of the salt on each of 4 serving plates. Nestle 3 of the egg shells into the salt on each plate.

Melt the butter in a 10- or 12-inch skillet over medium heat. Beat together the eggs, milk, and salt and pepper in a medium bowl and pour into the pan. Let the eggs set and then begin to lift and fold with a spatula to form soft curds. Remove the eggs from the pan while they are slightly undercooked.

Carefully spoon the scrambled eggs into the shells, topping one egg with ½ teaspoon of the caviar, one egg with the foie gras, and then the third egg with the shaved truffle.

# BURRATA WITH GRILLED PEACHES, DUCK PROSCIUTTO, MUSTARD GREENS, AND MÂCHE

This is one of our most popular first courses. A recent bride, Alex Carl (who was an actress on *Gossip Girl*), and her South African groom, Peter Campbell, brought the combination to us and we did the styling. The bride and groom are real foodies; they can both cook and they have great ideas. Not only is this a good-looking salad, it also holds up well. The stone fruit (we use peaches or nectarines) can be grilled in advance and plated with the prosciutto; then the burrata and greens are added and dressed right before service. Burrata—creamy soft curds of cheese encased in mozzarella—is the star and it works beautifully here. The dish hits all tastes and textures: the sweetness of the fruit contrasts with the saltiness of the prosciutto and the slightly bitter baby mustard greens; the burrata is luscious and creamy, while the mâche adds another soft texture; and one crisped piece of prosciutto adds a touch of crunch.

*Serves 4*

10 slices of duck prosciutto

16 peach wedges (3 to 4 peaches, depending on their size)

2 8-ounce balls of burrata cheese

2 cups baby mustard greens

2 cups mâche

Red sorrel leaves, for garnish

Peach Vinaigrette (page 108)

*(recipe continues)*

# WILD MUSHROOM SOUP

I believe that Jean-Georges Vongerichten was the first to serve soup in this manner when he opened his Jean-Georges restaurant on Central Park West. He would snip fresh herbs into the bottom of the soup plate and then pour the hot soup over the herbs tableside. Years later, we adapted the idea for a wedding on a small island off Maine: we perfectly plate mushrooms and herbs in the bottom of the bowl and set it in front of the guest. Then another waiter comes with a pitcher of hot soup and pours that into the bowl. It makes for a beautiful presentation. It's a very flavorful broth, but you can still see the mushrooms, and people just love that layer of service and the theater of a waiter finishing the dish right in front of them.

*Serves 4 (about 4 cups)*

3 pounds wild mushrooms or sliced button mushrooms

2 large shallots, chopped

2 garlic cloves, crushed

1 bunch of fresh thyme

1 bay leaf

2 quarts vegetable stock

2 tablespoons extra-virgin olive oil

8 ounces wild mushrooms (chanterelle, enoki, maitake, royal trumpet, or a mixture), trimmed and cut into bite-size pieces if large

¼ cup Madeira (optional)

Coarse salt and freshly ground black pepper

Fresh micro chives (or snipped regular chives) and cilantro flowers, for garnish (optional)

Put the mushrooms, shallots, garlic, thyme, bay leaf, and stock in a stock pot. Bring to a boil over high heat, then reduce the heat to medium-low and simmer gently until reduced by half, about 1½ hours. Line a sieve with two layers of rinsed and squeezed cheesecloth and set over a clean 3-quart pot. Pour in the broth and press on the vegetables to extract all the liquid; discard the solids. The broth can be made in advance and refrigerated for up to 2 days.

When ready to serve, make the wild mushrooms. In a deep 10- or 12-inch sauté pan, heat the oil over medium-high heat until just smoking. Add the mushrooms and cook, stirring, until cooked through and golden brown, 8 to 10 minutes.

Return the broth to medium heat to warm it and stir in the Madeira, if using, and salt and pepper to taste. Arrange 4 or 5 sautéed mushrooms at the bottom of each bowl and pour the broth over. Garnish with chives and cilantro flowers, if desired.

# POTATO LEEK SOUP WITH SLICED TRUFFLE AND FRIZZLED LEEKS

This is a luxurious soup with a lot of texture and flavor, yet it contains no cream—we never add any milk or cream to our soups. In addition to the leeks in the soup itself, which bring a wonderful sweetness to the broth, we first place sautéed leeks in the bowl and pour the soup around them. Then we top the soup with sliced truffle and a bit of frizzled leeks for crunch.

*Serves 6 (about 8 cups)*

Melt the butter in a 3-quart pot. Add the raw leeks, onion, and potato and stir until well coated with the butter. Sweat over medium-low heat until soft (do not let the vegetables brown), about 10 minutes.

Add the wine, increase the heat to medium, and simmer until the liquid is reduced by half, 7 to 10 minutes. Add the chicken stock and bring to a boil over high heat; then reduce the heat and simmer for 30 minutes. Puree the soup with an immersion blender until smooth, passing the soup through a fine-mesh sieve if you'd like it extra smooth. Add salt and pepper to taste.

To serve, place a small pile of soft julienned leeks in the center of the soup plate as a platform for the frizzled leeks and shaved truffles. Pour the soup around the pile of leeks. Top the leeks with a slice or two of black truffle and sprinkle with frizzled leeks. Drizzle lightly with truffle oil.

---

8 tablespoons (1 stick) unsalted butter

8 small or 5 large leeks, white parts only, thinly sliced (about 3 cups)

½ large onion, diced

1 russet potato, peeled and diced

1½ cups dry white wine

2 quarts chicken stock

Coarse salt and freshly ground black pepper

Soft Julienned Leeks (recipe opposite), for garnish

Shaved black truffle, for garnish

Frizzled leeks (see page 99), for garnish

Truffle oil, for garnish

# Soft Julienned Leeks

*Makes about 1 cup*

3 large leeks, white part only

1½ tablespoons unsalted butter

Cut the leeks in half lengthwise,
rinse well, and slice into a fine
julienne.

Melt the butter in an 8-inch skillet
over medium heat and add the
leeks. Stir to coat well with the
butter and continue to cook over
low heat until soft, but not browned,
about 10 minutes.

# SORREL SOUP

My chef originally developed this soup for a seven-hundred-guest glatt kosher wedding at the Park Avenue Armory for a very well-known family in New York City. They wanted really special food and we liked the idea of doing a sorrel soup, which is rustic and woodsy tasting and sort of esoteric. In the end they selected something a little more mainstream, but now the soup is on our menu anyway and it really is terrific.

It's an unusual dish with the provocative flavors of the pureed sorrel and apple. Many soups benefit from the sweetness of a little diced fruit. The garnish of smoked trout adds a nice punch of flavor and texture.

*Serves 6 (about 8 cups)*

---

1 tablespoon extra-virgin olive oil

1 Spanish onion, diced

1 Granny Smith apple, peeled and diced

1 leek, white and tender green parts, washed well and thinly sliced

1 large shallot, chopped

1½ teaspoons chopped garlic

1 cup dry white wine

6 cups chicken stock

½ cup heavy cream

4 bunches of sorrel (about 1½ pounds)

½ cup (packed) fresh basil leaves

4 tablespoons (½ stick) unsalted butter

Coarse salt

2 ounces smoked trout, cut into 12 small diamonds

Red-veined sorrel leaves, for garnish

Warm the oil in a 3-quart stockpot over medium-low heat. Add the onion, apple, leek, shallot, and garlic and sauté until the onion is translucent and the apple is tender, 7 to 10 minutes. Do not let them brown.

Add the wine, bring to a boil over medium-high heat, and cook until reduced by half, 7 to 10 minutes. Add the stock, cream, half of the sorrel, and the basil. Bring back to a boil, then lower the heat to medium-low and simmer until reduced by one-fourth, 30 to 35 minutes. Remove from the heat and let cool completely, about 30 minutes.

Pour three-quarters of the soup into a high-speed blender or a food processor. Pulse until smooth, then strain through a fine-mesh sieve into a clean 3-quart pot. Pour the remaining soup into the blender, add the remaining sorrel and the butter, and pulse until smooth. Strain through a fine-mesh sieve into the first batch of soup. Season with salt to taste if needed.

Reheat gently over low heat (do not let it boil, or the soup will turn dark) before serving. Divide among 6 bowls and garnish each with 2 diamonds of smoked trout and red-veined sorrel leaves.

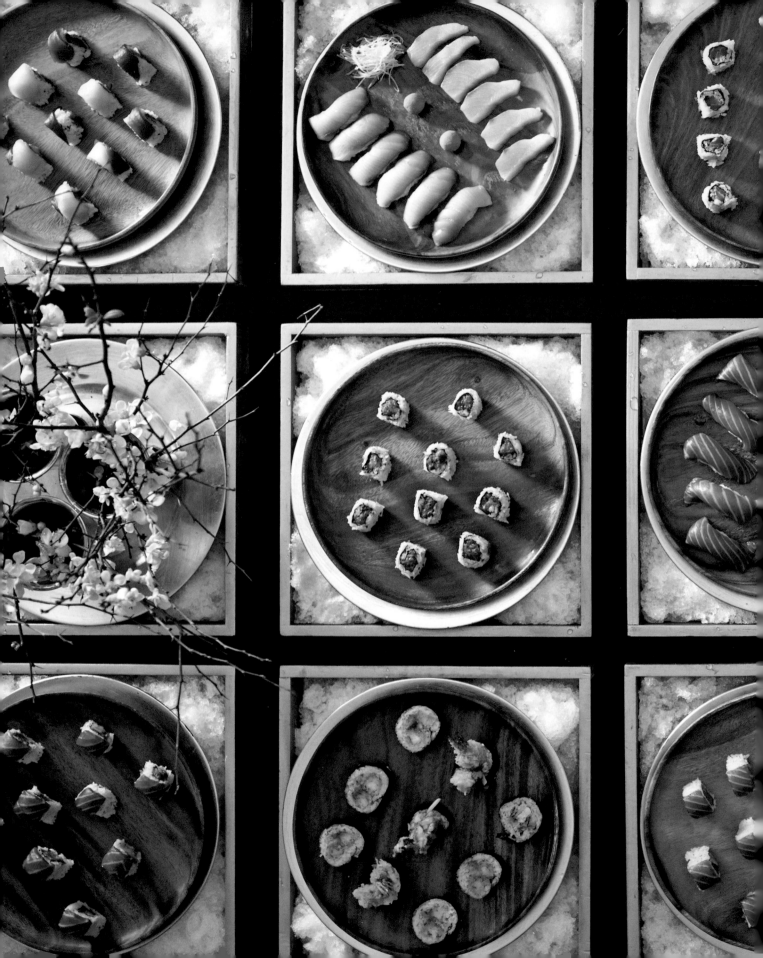

**SUSHI STATION** We designed this beautiful sushi display, with wooden platters set into a matrix of boxes filled with shaved ice, to keep the sushi cold. We put each kind of sushi on an individual plate.

The display is made of square trays that we fill with shaved ice; then we set a charger plate filled with sushi on top of each tray. You can make this at home from boxes in any size or configuration that you want.

# BUTTERNUT SQUASH RAVIOLI

We make these with wonton wrappers and steam them, so they puff up and are very light. This dish works well as a first course, but we also use it as a "silent" vegetarian entrée (see page 137). We serve these with a nice herb sauce on the side, often a basil sauce. Everyone loves them and they can be fired off fairly quickly if need be.

*Serves 4*

2½ cups diced peeled butternut squash (about ½ small)

¾ cup diced carrots

2 tablespoons extra-virgin olive oil

Sea salt

1 yellow onion, cut into thick wedges

2 garlic cloves

1½ teaspoons grated fresh ginger

1½ teaspoons chopped fresh sage

24 wonton wrappers

Basil Cream Sauce (recipe follows)

Shaved Parmesan cheese, for garnish

Preheat the oven to 350°F.

In a large bowl, toss the squash, carrots, and 1 tablespoon of the oil. Sprinkle with about ½ teaspoon salt and toss again. Spread in a single layer on a baking sheet. Toss the onion wedges and garlic in the same bowl with the remaining 1 tablespoon oil and a pinch of salt. Spread on a second baking sheet. Roast until soft but not browned, 35 to 40 minutes.

Transfer the roasted vegetables along with the ginger and sage to a food processor and puree until very smooth, scraping down the sides once or twice. Set aside to cool completely.

*(recipe continues)*

Lay 12 wonton wrappers on a work surface and brush the edges with water. Place a ½-tablespoon mound of filling in the center of each and top with a second wrapper. Press the edges to seal, making sure to remove trapped air. Cut with a 2-inch square cutter to trim. (If you have leftover filling, save it for another use or make more ravioli.)

Fill a pot large enough to snugly hold a bamboo steamer halfway with water and bring to a boil over high heat. Reduce the heat to medium and set a bamboo steamer on top. Working in batches, steam the ravioli until the wrappers are translucent, 5 to 6 minutes.

To plate, spoon some of the warm basil cream sauce onto individual serving plates and arrange 3 ravioli on each. Top with shaved Parmesan.

# Basil Cream Sauce

*Makes about 2 cups*

---

1 tablespoon extra-virgin olive oil

½ cup diced onion

2 garlic cloves, minced

1 cup dry white wine

2 cups vegetable stock

¼ cup heavy cream

Coarse salt and freshly ground black pepper

1 cup (packed) basil leaves


Heat the oil in a medium saucepan over medium heat. Add the onion and garlic and sauté until soft but not browned, 2 to 3 minutes. Add the wine and deglaze the pan. Continue to cook until reduced by half.

Add the vegetable stock and heavy cream and reduce until the sauce coats the back of a spoon, 10 to 12 minutes. Add salt and pepper to taste and set aside to cool.

Pour the sauce into a blender or food processor along with the basil leaves and puree until smooth. When ready to serve, return the sauce to the pan and warm gently over low heat. Do not let the sauce come to a boil, as it will turn brown.

# The American Chef Corps

The American Chef Corps is a network of chefs from across the country who serve as a resource to the U.S. Department of State in its efforts to incorporate culinary engagement in its public diplomacy efforts. Created in 2012 in partnership with the James Beard Foundation, the corps is part of an initiative developed under then Secretary of State Hillary Clinton. Her rationale, she said, is that "food isn't traditionally thought of as a diplomatic tool, but I think it's the oldest diplomatic tool. Sharing a meal can help people transcend boundaries and build bridges in a way that nothing else can."

Secretary Clinton wanted to update the food that's served throughout the diplomatic corps to reflect the best of American cuisine. So the State Department invited more than eighty chefs from all over the country to participate in whatever ways were meaningful. I was asked to cater and design the kickoff party at the State Department that announced the formation of the Chefs Corps, and another reception held in preparation for the 2015 World Food Expo in Milan.

I am very proud to be a part of the Chef Corps, which includes top chefs from all over the country, among them José Andrés, Dan Barber, Rick Bayless, April Bloomfield, Marcus Samuelsson, and Ming Tsai. It's a great program and it really brings home the importance of learning about other cultures and sharing ours through the global world of food.

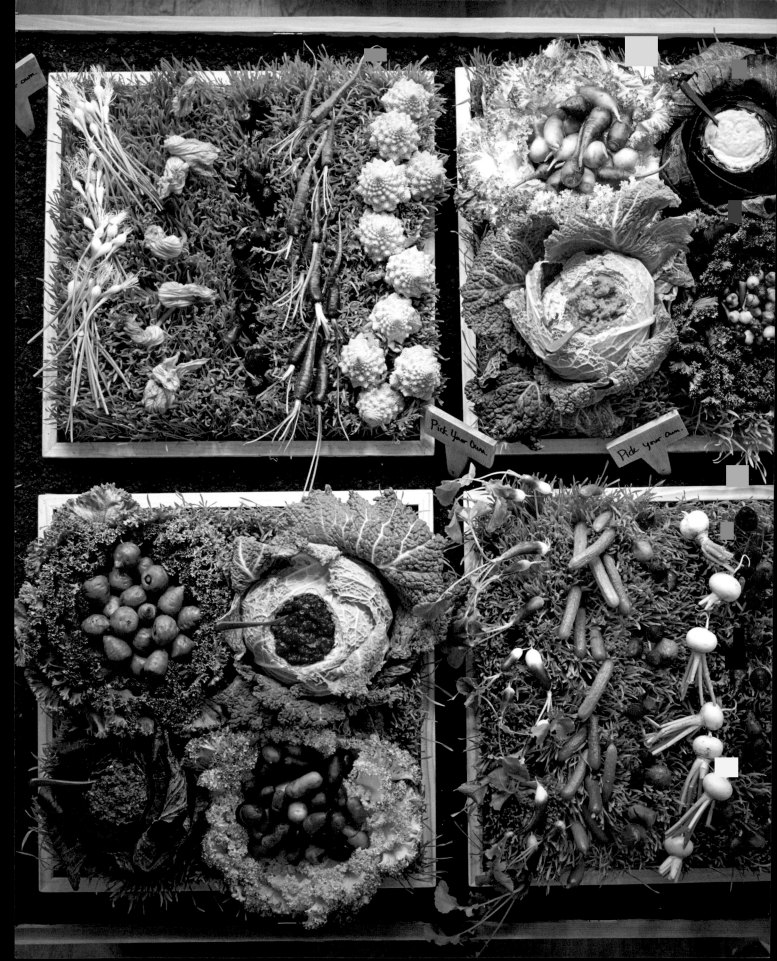

Pick Your Own.

Pick Your Own.

## CRUDITÉ FIELD

Martha Stewart's American Made celebrates artisanal products made across the country through an annual award program and conference held during its first two years at Grand Central Terminal in New York City. We conceived this display for the event's second year to tie in with the program's theme of farm-to-table foods and other items made by hand. It's a "back to the land" take on crudités that's literally grab and go, as if guests are picking vegetables from the field.

We construct a series of plywood boxes: a large box to hold the soil and a matrix of smaller boxes for the vegetable beds. All manner of vegetables—carrots, radishes, cucumbers, and even potatoes—spring up from the field of wheat grass, while hollowed-out Savoy and red cabbages and ornamental kales make natural serving bowls.

The amazing variety of heirloom vegetables available now means this beautiful display isn't limited to the summer months—there's a rainbow of different colors in winter vegetables, too, and many can be found in "baby" sizes. Visit your local farmer's market to find the best of what's in season. The veggies in the photo come from Chef's Garden, a wonderful resource (see Sources, page 251).

We've done versions of our field of crudités for many other parties and events since then. It's perfect for outdoor parties and also makes a great table centerpiece for a rustic-themed wedding. We buy wheatgrass flats from local flower shops and push bamboo skewers of vegetables into the grass.

# OPEN-FACED LOBSTER RAVIOLI

This is a remake of lobster ravioli with an almost deconstructed approach—you get to see all the beautiful ingredients and make your own decision how much pasta you want to have with your meal. This is an elegant first course that is very easy to make at home. Store-bought fresh pasta sheets work perfectly and steamed lobster can be purchased from your fishmonger.

*Serves 4*

**For the Pasta Sheets:**

2 large eggs

2 cups all-purpose flour

**For the Fennel Confit:**

2 fennel bulbs, cored and thinly sliced

2 cups extra-virgin olive oil

**For the Lobster:**

2 lemons, halved

½ cup coarse salt

2 1½-pound live lobsters

1 pound (4 sticks) unsalted butter, cubed

**For the Sautéed Spinach:**

1 tablespoon extra-virgin olive oil

1 shallot, minced

2 garlic cloves, minced

4 cups spinach, stems removed

Coarse salt and freshly ground black pepper

**For Serving:**

White Wine–Lemon Sauce (page 126)

Chervil leaves or fresh flat-leaf parsley sprigs, for garnish

**PASTA SHEETS**

Place the eggs and 1 tablespoon of water in the bowl of a stand mixer fitted with the paddle attachment. Lightly beat the eggs. With the motor running, slowly add the flour, ½ cup at a time, until the dough just comes together (you may not need all the flour). Turn off the mixer and exchange the paddle for the dough hook. Continue to mix the dough until smooth and elastic, about 5 minutes. Form the dough into a ball and wrap it in plastic wrap. Let sit at room temperature for about 30 minutes to allow the gluten to relax.

**FENNEL CONFIT**

Meanwhile, place the fennel in a medium saucepan and pour in the oil. Cook the fennel—submerged in the oil—over medium-low heat until completely tender, about 30 minutes. Remove with a slotted spoon and transfer to paper towels to drain before plating.

**PASTA**

Roll out the pasta. Run the dough through a pasta machine, beginning at the largest number and ending with the thickness you prefer. Run the dough through each number twice. Once the pasta is rolled to your desired thickness it can either be cut into squares and frozen between layers of parchment paper and placed in a plastic bag or cooked while the lobster is poaching. Do not cook the pasta ahead of time; frozen pasta can be cooked as described below.

**LOBSTER**

Prepare an ice bath in a bowl large enough to hold both lobsters. In a lobster pot or large stockpot with a lid, bring 2 to 3 gallons of water to a boil over high heat. Squeeze in the lemon juice and add the salt. Quickly place the lobsters in the water, cover, and cook for 7 minutes. Transfer the lobsters to the ice bath.

Use kitchen shears to cut the shells. Carefully remove the meat from the claws and the tails, leaving the meat intact. Cut each tail in half lengthwise, removing the vein that runs down its center. Reserve any remaining lobster meat for another use.

*(recipe continues)*

In a medium saucepan, bring ¼ cup water to a slow boil over medium heat. Reduce the heat to low and whisk in the butter. Continue to whisk until the butter has melted and emulsified (do not let the butter foam).

Add the lobster claws and tails to the butter and poach until the meat is no longer translucent and has just turned white and pink, 5 to 7 minutes.

### SAUTÉED SPINACH

Heat the oil in a large skillet over medium heat. Add the shallot and garlic and sauté until translucent, about 5 minutes. Add all of the spinach and sauté, stirring constantly, until evenly cooked, 2 to 3 minutes. Take care not to overcook as spinach discolors quickly. Season to taste with salt and pepper.

### ASSEMBLE

Cut the rolled pasta dough into four 4-inch squares and three 3-inch squares. Bring a large pot of salted water to a boil over high heat. Add the squares to the boiling water and cook for only 2 to 3 minutes, until al dente. Drain.

### SERVE

Drizzle some of the white wine–lemon sauce on each plate and place 1 large pasta square in the center. Top with a ½ lobster tail and arrange a spoonful of the fennel and the spinach on either side. Place the smaller pasta square to partially cover a bit of the tail and arrange the lobster claw on top. Garnish with chervil or parsley sprigs.

# White Wine–Lemon Sauce

*Makes about 1½ cups*

---

1 cup extra-virgin olive oil

⅓ cup dry white wine

Juice of 1 lemon (about 3 tablespoons)

Coarse salt

In a small bowl, whisk together the oil, wine, lemon juice, and salt to taste.

# LEMON-SCENTED QUINOA

Like the Ratatouille (page 132), this is another vegetable-forward dish that works well as a first course or a main dish. I love to take advantage of the wide variety of colorful heirloom vegetables available today—the candy-striped beets, the beautiful watermelon radishes. Peeling thin strips of asparagus and carrots and letting them curl in ice water adds a modern, fresh look to the plate.

Quinoa and grains have definitely been rediscovered and are a great addition to a salad or a salad alternative. Shaving the vegetables is an easy technique that elevates their presentation. This dish has a lot of substance. It's filling, but still has the lightness and crisp texture of a salad—and it can be plated ahead of time without wilting as a salad would.

*Serves 8 as a first course; 4 as a main*

**For the Quinoa:**

2 cups quinoa

1 quart vegetable stock or water

Grated zest and juice of 2 lemons

**For the Vegetables:**

1 bunch of asparagus, thinly shaved with a vegetable peeler

3 heirloom carrots, 1 orange, 1 yellow, and 1 purple, thinly sliced lengthwise on a mandoline

1 watermelon radish, thinly sliced crosswise

6 baby candy-striped beets, cut in half and thinly sliced on a mandoline

6 baby yellow beets, cut in half and thinly sliced on a mandoline

6 jarred baby artichokes, cut into quarters

1 tablespoon grated lemon zest

¼ cup extra-virgin olive oil

Freshly ground black pepper

Caramelized Shallot and Lemon Vinaigrette (recipe follows)

Bibb lettuce, for serving

## QUINOA

In a medium heavy saucepan over medium-high heat, combine the quinoa and vegetable stock (if using water, add 1 teaspoon coarse salt). Bring to a boil, reduce the heat to low, and cover. Once most of the liquid is absorbed, about 15 minutes, test for doneness and fluff with a fork. Add the lemon zest and juice.

*(recipe continues)*

**PERFECT PRESENTATION**

**BAGELS AND LOX STATION** This is my interpretation of the classic deli case by Russ & Daughters, the generations-old smoked fish purveyor on Manhattan's Lower East Side. Three tiers hold the condiments, whole white fish and smoked salmon, and the bagels (which are stacked on dowels in the rear). This is a perfect buffet to serve before an early Sunday afternoon wedding or as part of a brunch-time event.

# RATATOUILLE

I love the deconstructed, free-form look of this dish, as if everything was dropped into the bowl and just happened to fall in really nice places. It doesn't appear fussed over by a chef, but is arranged in a pleasing, seemingly accidental way. The vegetables are all well caramelized to provide deep, rich flavor. The stems and roots are left on for a great farm-to-table effect. The polenta makes this a hearty first course that works equally well as a vegetarian main.

*Serves 8 as a first course; 4 as a main*

**For the Polenta:**

1 quart vegetable stock or water

1 cup polenta

Grated zest of 2 lemons

2 teaspoons chopped fresh thyme

2 teaspoons coarse salt

½ teaspoon freshly ground black pepper

Nonstick cooking spray

Olive oil, for frying

**For the Tomato Broth:**

1 tablespoon extra-virgin olive oil

3 shallots, roughly chopped

3 garlic cloves, crushed and roughly chopped

½ cup dry white wine

1 14-ounce can tomatoes, diced or whole peeled

1½ cups vegetable stock

1 bunch of fresh thyme

2 bay leaves

Coarse salt and freshly ground black pepper

**For the Vegetables:**

4 yellow pattypan squash, halved

4 baby eggplants, halved

1 zucchini, cut into ½-inch rounds

4 cipollini onions, halved

8 maitake mushrooms

4 baby tomatoes on the vine, halved

4 ramps

4 spring onions (red or white), halved

Coarse salt and freshly ground black pepper

1 tablespoon extra-virgin olive oil

## POLENTA

Pour the vegetable stock into a medium heavy saucepan (if using water instead of stock, add 1 teaspoon kosher salt). Bring to a boil over medium heat and stream in the polenta while stirring constantly. Continue to stir until the polenta is completely combined and no lumps remain. Reduce the heat to medium-low and continue to stir until the polenta thickens. Cook, stirring every 10 minutes or so, until very thick, 30 to 45 minutes.

Add the lemon zest, thyme, and salt and pepper.

Line a baking sheet with parchment paper sprayed with nonstick spray. Spoon the polenta, about ⅓ cup at a time, into free-form shapes on the parchment. Refrigerate at least 2 hours or overnight.

## TOMATO BROTH

Heat the oil in a medium saucepan over medium heat. Add the shallots and garlic and sauté just until aromatic. Deglaze the pan with the white wine and continue to cook until the liquid is reduced by half.

Add the tomatoes, stock, thyme, and bay leaves. Bring the broth back to a boil; reduce the heat to low. Simmer for about 1 hour, then season to taste with salt and pepper. Strain the broth through a fine-mesh strainer into a medium bowl, discarding the solids.

Heat a 10- or 12-inch skillet over medium-high heat and fill it a quarter of the way with olive oil. Fry the polenta on both sides until golden brown, 1 to 2 minutes per side. Drain on paper towels.

## VEGETABLES

Season all of the vegetables with salt and pepper. Heat a large sauté pan over high heat and add the oil. Reduce the heat to medium-high and, working in batches if necessary, give the vegetable pieces a nice hard sear by pressing them down with a spatula. Do not flip until the first side is a deep golden brown. The ramps will take only a few seconds in the pan to soften; do not overcook. Sear the maitake mushrooms a few minutes longer than the rest of the vegetables.

## SERVE

Return the broth to the saucepan to reheat. Place one piece of polenta on the plate and assemble the vegetables on top. Pour the broth around the bottom of the plate just before serving.

**MATRIX BUFFET** Our matrix buffet is inspired by farmer's market displays. We use individual square trays.

This buffet is a very inexpensive way to create a big wow, as vegetables are reasonably priced and little labor is involved in this easy preparation.

# Vegetarian Should Not Be an Afterthought

You have to offer a vegetarian option at any dinner. You may think none of your guests are vegetarians, but then you'll find that someone's doing a cleanse. We offer a vegetarian option for every course of every dinner. We have done an eight-course tasting dinner, and every course that was not already vegetarian had a vegetarian option.

We call these "silent" vegetarian options because they are not listed on the official menu. More often than not, when we take the order at the table, asking, "Would you like the branzino or the short ribs?" someone will say, "Oh, I'm vegan." So we always have the option available and we always make the dishes vegan. We try to make them gluten free as well, so that we cover as many bases as possible. If we do the branzino with toasted panko, it's not gluten free. And you'll often get someone who says there can't be any oil, any salt, not a speck of butter, I'm allergic to shallots, garlic . . . You can't be a short-order kitchen when you're serving seven hundred people who all want their dinner at the same time. Welcome to my world.

# LIGHTLY BREADED BRANZINO

This is our most popular fish entrée. Branzino is a delicious, light fish that is known by many names along its native Mediterranean coast, including sea bass and loup de mer. When cooking fish, the key word is moist, and this preparation is designed to deliver a perfect piece to every plate. It also makes serving fish to guests in your home super easy.

First we double-stack the two sides of the fillet into a single piece. That gives us a thicker piece of fish to work with and makes it more practical to cook properly for a large group. We then coat the fish with panko, sear it on the stovetop, and finish it in the oven with a more gentle heat. We serve it with a selection of steamed summer vegetables, such as zucchini, yellow squash, carrots, and peeled, sautéed small tomatoes.

The panko crumbs add a nice color to the white fish as well as crunch, and help to keep it moist. The tomato confit gives the dish a bright spot of color and flavor without adding any cream or butter.

*Serves 4*

Nonstick cooking spray

8 4-ounce branzino fillets

Coarse salt

2 cups panko

½ cup extra-virgin olive oil

¼ cup grapeseed oil

Lemon-Ponzu Beurre Blanc (page 144)

Tomato Confit (page 143)

Preheat the oven to 350°F. Line a baking sheet with parchment paper and spray with nonstick spray.

Place 2 fillets on top of each other—skin sides together—to make a thicker fillet; repeat with the remaining fish for 4 thick fillets. Season with salt.

In a small bowl, mix the panko with the olive oil to create a slightly damp mixture that will stick together and to the fish but retain a crumbly texture. Press the panko mixture onto the top of the fillets.

In a large sauté pan over high heat, heat the grapeseed oil until almost smoking. Reduce the heat to medium, place the fillets in the pan crumb side down and cook, without moving them, until golden brown, about 3 minutes.

Place the fish, crumb side up, on the prepared baking sheet and bake until just cooked through, 7 to 8 minutes.

Top the fish with a dollop of tomato confit. Serve with the beurre blanc and a selection of vegetables in season, simply prepared.

---

## HOW MANY CHOICES SHOULD I OFFER?

There is always a question as to whether guests should be offered a single entrée or given a choice, to be ordered when they are first seated for dinner. You always need a vegan option. But beyond that, my response to the "how many entrées?" question is: What is your first instinct? If it's "I am serving lamb to all my guests," that's what you'll do. If you say, "How could I ever offer my guests only one entrée?" then there's your answer. In addition to a vegan option on request, you can always have a few fish or beef options for silent requests (in other words, the guest needs to ask if there is an alternative), depending on what the main entrée is.

# SEARED CRISPY HALIBUT

Halibut is a versatile and almost universally liked fish. It holds up well for large groups because it is thick. The trick with halibut, like a lot of fish, is to do less to it. Starting at our own kitchens, we just marinate it in a lot of olive oil and then sear it over superhigh heat—it gets a nice caramelized brown crust, but is still raw in the middle. Then the fish is reheated at the party to cook through right before it's served. And that's something you can do with fish at home, too—sear it over high heat on the stovetop earlier in the day, then finish it in the oven just before serving your guests.

There's an incredible amount of thought behind the plating of this dish, yet it's all very simple. Sautéed greens form a base for the fish—they will keep the fish warm and moist as the plate travels from the kitchen to the table. A little lemon-ponzu beurre blanc is spooned to the side. We slice fingerling potatoes into coins instead of roasting them whole; it makes them look fancier. Carrots are available in beautiful colors now and we leave the tops on to emphasize the "farm-to-table" freshness of the food. Serving the peas in their pods looks great, but eating them makes extra work for the guests, so we use only two pods. The accompaniments are simply steamed or roasted. Choose the best of what's in season to accompany your fish.

The halibut is topped with one of my favorite ingredients. Tomato Confit (page 143) is a home run on almost any plate. Just a spoonful adds incredible flavor, color, and texture. I can't say enough about this—make a batch and keep it in your refrigerator; you'll use it all the time.

Grapeseed oil has a very high smoking point, so you can get the pan hot enough to sear the fish. When placing the fish in the pan, make sure you're searing the "pretty side" by placing the fillets skin side up.

*Serves 4*

---

| | |
|---|---|
| Nonstick cooking spray | Coarse salt and freshly ground white pepper |
| 2 tablespoons grapeseed oil | Lemon-Ponzu Beurre Blanc (page 144) |
| 1½ pounds skinless, boneless halibut fillets, in 4 pieces | Tomato Confit (page 143) |

Preheat the oven to 350°F. Line a baking sheet with parchment paper and spray with nonstick spray.

Heat the grapeseed oil in a 10- or 12-inch sauté pan over medium heat until hot. Generously season the fillets with salt and pepper and place carefully in the pan, skin side up. Cook without moving until golden brown and crispy, about 3 minutes.

Place the fish, browned side up, on the prepared baking sheet and bake until just cooked through, 5 to 7 minutes.

Top the fish with a dollop of tomato confit. Serve with the beurre blanc and a selection of vegetables in season, simply prepared.

# MY THREE FAVORITE SAUCES FOR FISH

Our clients eat out almost every night and one of the most common remarks we hear during the menu planning is that they don't want to feel heavy at the end of the meal. There may be dancing or a program of speeches after dinner, and they want their guests to be full, but not ready to go to sleep.

Guests who choose fish are especially looking for a lighter meal, and that's why it's important to pair fish dishes with sauces that are full of flavor, but not a lot of fat and sugar.

Salsa Verde, a combination of herbs, garlic, lemon juice, and a touch of red pepper, also adds color and flavor, but it's a light sauce, with very little oil.

We have three sauces for every guest and place setting. One client liked all three sauces at a tasting, so we made plates to hold the sauces.

# TOMATO CONFIT

*Makes about 2 cups*

---

4 large, meaty tomatoes (such as Roma), about ½ pound

Extra-virgin olive oil

3 garlic cloves

1 tablespoon coriander seeds

1 tablespoon white peppercorns

Coarse salt

Preheat the oven to 250°F.

Halve the tomatoes, core them, and remove the seeds. Place cut side down in a baking dish just large enough to hold them (about 8 inches). Add enough olive oil to come two-thirds of the way up the tomatoes.

Make a cheesecloth sachet containing the garlic, coriander, and white peppercorns and place in the dish. Sprinkle the tomatoes generously with salt.

Cover the dish tightly with aluminum foil and bake for 2 hours. Remove from the oven and discard the foil. Pull off the tomato skins and let the tomatoes cool in the dish, about ½ hour.

If not using the confit immediately, transfer the tomatoes to a lidded jar and pour in the oil from the pan. Add more oil to cover the tomatoes, if needed. Store in the refrigerator for up to 2 months.

# POACHED GIANT TIGER PRAWNS

1 cup dry white wine

1 lemon, sliced

2 bay leaves

¾ cup coarse salt

8 black peppercorns, cracked

8 giant tiger prawns (13–15 count per pound), or 16 jumbo shrimp, shells on and tails intact

Spicy Cocktail Sauce (at right)

Prepare an ice water bath. In a 5-quart pot, combine 6 cups water with the wine, lemon slices, bay leaves, salt, and peppercorns. Bring the mixture to a boil over medium heat; then reduce to a simmer. Add the prawns and cook until they are no longer transparent and have just turned white and pink, 4 to 5 minutes. Take care not to overcook. With a spider or a large slotted spoon, transfer the prawns to the ice water bath, then drain on paper towels.

Peel the prawns while holding them under cold running water. Still under running water, use a paring knife to make a shallow slit down the middle of the back of each prawn to expose the black vein. Lift out the vein with the tip of the knife and wipe it off with a paper towel.

Serve the prawns with the sliced strip steak, a selection of seasonal vegetables, and the spicy cocktail sauce and beef sauce of your choice on the side.

## Spicy Cocktail Sauce

*Makes 2 cups*

---

2 garlic cloves

1 shallot

⅓ cup (packed) roasted red peppers

3 tablespoons honey

1 teaspoon Tabasco sauce

3 tablespoons freshly squeezed lemon juice

1½ teaspoons Worcestershire sauce

1 cup ketchup

⅔ cup prepared horseradish, drained

Coarse salt and freshly ground black pepper

Place the garlic and shallot in a blender or mini food processor and pulse until pureed. Add the roasted red peppers and pulse until chopped and combined. Transfer the mixture to a medium bowl and add the honey, Tabasco, lemon juice, Worcestershire sauce, ketchup, and horseradish. Stir to combine and add salt and pepper to taste.

## RAW BAR BOAT

I grew up in a boating family and spent a lot of time on the water. We get a lot of requests for raw bars and, to me, the beauty of the raw bar is all about how you display it. Back in the day there would be a large Plexiglas bowl, maybe with a big carved-ice seahorse in the middle, illuminated in blue. Spanky's Raw Bar on Nantucket always set up its raw bars in small wooden boats—and we once set up a raw bar in a client's rowboat. All of which led me to think of doing a carved-ice boat.

Okamoto Studio Custom Ice carved the boat, which sits in a tray of shaved ice, and all the food—clams and oysters; cocktail sauce, horseradish, and mignonette sauce; crab claws and shrimp—is arranged on ice in the boat.

PERFECT PRESENTATION

# BEEF TWO WAYS

Short ribs are a chef's best friend because there's no such thing as overcooking them. In catering, especially with large dinner parties, you don't always know your timing. Sometimes a speech goes long or people are dancing, so you look for dishes that you can hold without sacrificing taste.

This is a great dish for home entertaining because much of the work can be done ahead of time. The tenderloin is marinated overnight and, if you wish, you can prepare the short ribs the day before, up to the last step of reducing the braising liquid. It's also a reasonably inexpensive dish, with the exception of the amount of red wine needed to make a really good sauce.

We serve this with roasted kale (purple, variegated, and green) and roasted sweet potato wedges.

*Serves 4 to 6*

# BRAISED SHORT RIBS

| | |
|---|---|
| 3½ pounds boneless beef short ribs | 1 celery stalk, cut into 1-inch pieces |
| Coarse salt and freshly ground black pepper | 1½ 750-ml bottles of dry red wine |
| ¼ cup extra-virgin olive oil | 1 teaspoon crushed black peppercorns |
| 5 garlic cloves | 5 thyme sprigs |
| 2 large sweet onions | 1 bay leaf |
| 1 carrot, cut into 1-inch pieces | 1½ quarts beef stock |
| | 1 3-ounce container beef or veal demi-glace |

Preheat the oven to 300°F. Season the short ribs with salt and pepper. In a Dutch oven, heat the olive oil over medium heat until almost smoking. Add the ribs and sear until well browned, 4 to 5 minutes on each side. Remove the meat from the pan and set aside.

Add the garlic, onions, carrot, and celery to the same pot and cook over medium heat until lightly browned, 5 to 7 minutes. Pour the wine over the vegetables and simmer until reduced by half.

Add the peppercorns, thyme, bay leaf, stock, and demi-glace and return the short ribs to the pot. Bring to a boil and turn off the heat. Add salt and pepper to taste. Cover the pot tightly and braise in the oven for 2½ hours or until the ribs are fork-tender.

Transfer the ribs to a platter, strain the braising liquid, and return both the ribs and the strained liquid to the pan. Let cool completely, about ½ hour.

Once cool, trim the ribs of any excess fat or gristle and portion onto serving plates. Skim the fat from the braising liquid and reduce over low heat to a sauce-like consistency, about 8 minutes. Drizzle over the ribs.

# BEEF TENDERLOIN

1 2-pound, center-cut
tenderloin, trimmed
and tied by the butcher

1 cup minced shallots

½ cup minced garlic

4 fresh thyme sprigs

2 tablespoons extra-
virgin olive oil plus
more for marinating

Coarse salt and freshly
ground black pepper

Place the beef in a pan just big enough to hold it
(a 9 × 13-inch pan usually works well). Scatter
the shallots and garlic over the meat and add the
thyme. Fill the pan with enough olive oil to cover
the beef, cover the pan with plastic wrap, and
refrigerate overnight.

Bring the meat up to room temperature 1 hour
before cooking. When ready to cook, remove the
beef from the pan and wipe off the excess oil,
garlic, and shallots. Season the meat with salt
and pepper.

Preheat the oven to 450°F. Heat the 2 tablespoons
oil in a large ovenproof sauté pan over high
heat. Add the meat and brown it completely
on all sides, 4 to 5 minutes per side. Move the
sauté pan to the oven and roast until an instant-
read thermometer reads 120°F for rare, 10 to
20 minutes (the meat will continue to cook while
resting).

Let the meat rest for 10 minutes before carving
into ½-inch slices, taking care to remove any
butcher's twine.

**BURGERS AND FRITES BUFFET** It's such simple food—burgers and fries—but we elevate it to new levels with this look.

A display has a lot to do with selecting interesting containers to hold the food, and placing them at different levels and heights so that everything can be seen, yet is still easy to reach. We serve three different kinds of burgers (a veggie burger, a beef burger, and a short-rib burger) and a variety of fries (classic pommes frites, spicy Cajun, decadent truffle-Parmesan, and fried zucchini). The condiments and accompaniments fill the front row.

And once again we supersize cones here, which we dreamed up when my chef said, "I wish I could just supersize these mini cones."

# GINGER-SCENTED ROASTED CAULIFLOWER

Certain New York food moments are great; they're just quintessentially reflective of the city. Like when mac 'n' cheese became so big as an entrée that the fanciest restaurants were serving it for obscene amounts of money. Some famous actor would be quoted in the press saying that his favorite restaurant doesn't even have mac 'n' cheese on the menu but they'll make it for him every time. As if it's a culinary achievement? It's like the emperor's new clothes, and I'm all for it.

So I loved it when a few years ago restaurants started calling a slab of cauliflower taken from the center of the head a "cauliflower T-bone." Because now that you call it a T-bone, it's $45 on your menu. My wife is always trying to figure out ways to get our teenage daughter to eat more vegetables, so I serve her a cauliflower T-bone. Now we've put it on our menu as a vegetarian entrée, silent request (see page 137), and it's gluten free, which has become a common request.

You have to start with a nice center cut from the cauliflower. We brush it with good olive oil and powdered ginger and then roast it in a hot oven until it's charred, but not burnt, and soft and caramelized. We add a little broth (vegetable broth or our Wild Mushroom Soup, page 111) and some vegetables around it, in this case a roasted spring onion and three roasted candy-striped beets. All of a sudden that plate looks pretty sexy.

*Serves 4*

1 large head of cauliflower

¼ cup extra-virgin olive oil

2 tablespoons powdered ginger

2 teaspoons coarse salt

Freshly ground white pepper (optional)

Preheat the oven to 475°F.

Remove the leaves from the cauliflower but keep the stem intact. With a large, sharp knife, slice the cauliflower in ½- to ¾-inch-thick slices vertically from the top down through the stem.

Liberally brush both sides of the cauliflower "steaks" with the olive oil. In a small bowl, mix the powdered ginger and salt and sprinkle on both sides of each steak.

Arrange the steaks in a single layer on a baking sheet and roast until the bottom is golden brown, 15 to 20 minutes. Turn the steaks over and roast until cooked to the desired doneness, about 20 minutes more. Season with additional salt and pepper. if desired.

# CARROT WELLINGTON

As people eat less meat, chefs at many of the hottest restaurants are presenting menus that are vegetable forward, where vegetables that were once destined only for the soup pot are now the star of the plate. One such chef is John Fraser, and a version of this dish is a centerpiece of his menu at the downtown Manhattan restaurant Narcissa. Here, the concept of that old standby beef Wellington, a filet coated with mushrooms and wrapped in puff pastry, becomes completely modern when carrots replace the meat.

We serve this with Brussels sprout leaves that are blanched and then lightly sautéed in olive oil with minced shallots and a sprinkle of sea salt. A drizzle of balsamic syrup is added on the plate. Any side salad of sturdy greens in season would be appropriate here.

*Serves 4*

---

1½ pounds carrots, scrubbed and cut into 4-inch sticks

Coarse salt and freshly ground black pepper

5 tablespoons extra-virgin olive oil

3 thyme sprigs

12 ounces cremini mushrooms, roughly chopped

1 shallot, finely chopped

¼ cup dry white wine

1 tablespoon fresh tarragon, chopped

All-purpose flour, for dusting

1 sheet store-bought puff pastry, thawed if frozen

1 large egg

Preheat the oven to 400°F.

Set a steamer basket in a 3-quart saucepan, fill with water to reach just below the basket, and bring to a boil over high heat. Place the carrots in the basket and steam until tender, about 10 minutes.

Transfer the carrots to a 9 × 13-inch baking dish, season with salt and pepper, drizzle with 2 tablespoons of the olive oil, and add the thyme sprigs. Roast, turning occasionally, until the carrots are lightly caramelized and a bit wrinkled, about 30 minutes.

Pulse the mushrooms in a food processor until finely chopped. Heat the remaining 3 tablespoons olive oil in an 8-inch skillet over medium heat and add the mushrooms. Cook, stirring, until all the moisture is gone and the mushrooms begin to brown. Add the shallot and continue to cook until fragrant and soft. Add the white wine and cook until the liquid evaporates. Remove the pan from the heat and stir in the tarragon. Let cool completely, about 15 minutes.

Dust a clean work surface with flour, unfold the sheet of puff pastry, and roll it to a 16 × 12-inch rectangle. Spread the mushroom mixture over the surface, leaving a 1-inch border all around. Stack the carrots in 2 layers in the center, down the length of the pastry, and then roll the long edge snugly up and over the carrots. Place on a baking sheet, seam side down. Beat the egg with 1 tablespoon water and brush generously over the pastry. Bake until golden brown, about 25 minutes.

Use a sharp serrated knife to carve the Wellington into 1- to 2-inch slices. It will help keep the puff pastry from being compressed.

# RACK OF LAMB

These are big-eye Colorado lamb chops as opposed to the smaller New Zealand variety. They're delicious and a nice portion size. We pair the meat with tri-colored snow peas lightly dressed with a lemon vinaigrette, leaving the stems on to give them that "just picked from the garden" look. It's a very simple touch, yet it really makes the plate. The lamb is so rich that it's best paired with a light vegetable side. We serve the Salsa Verde (page 144) separately, because the plate is much more attractive without it. Plus this allows diners to add only as much sauce as they want, where they want it. (Personally, I slather on that sauce because I love salsa verde.)

Note that the meat needs to be marinated overnight. This makes it much more tender and less gamey. We submerge the meat in olive oil as we do with all our meats to tenderize and improve its flavor.

*Serves 4*

---

2 racks of lamb, preferably Colorado lamb (have your butcher French the bones and remove the fat cap)

2 garlic cloves, finely chopped

1 shallot, finely chopped

6 thyme sprigs

1 cup extra-virgin olive oil

1 cup white wine

Coarse salt

Salsa Verde (page 144)

Pat the lamb dry and place in a baking pan just large enough to hold the meat. Scatter the garlic, shallot, and thyme over the meat, then pour the oil and wine over all. The meat should be completely submerged. Cover the pan with plastic wrap and refrigerate overnight.

Bring the meat up to room temperature at least 1 hour before cooking. When ready to cook, remove the meat from the marinade and wipe clean. Salt the meat generously.

Preheat the oven to 350°F.

Heat a dry, heavy 12-inch ovenproof sauté pan over high heat until it's almost smoking. Add the meat and sear on all sides, then transfer the pan to the oven and roast until an instant-read thermometer inserted diagonally into the center of the meat reads 120°F, 20 to 30 minutes. Let the meat rest for 10 minutes before separating into chops (the meat will continue to cook to medium-rare).

Slice into chops and serve with seasonal vegetables and the salsa verde on the side.

## WILD MUSHROOM BUFFET

I am enamored with all things mushrooms: how they grow from the forest floor, their earthy flavors, and their exotic shapes. This display is inspired by how mushrooms grow in the woods—often on a fallen log. Instead of a table, we use a log to hold the food. All manner of edible wild mushrooms are set on the log as decor, while wooden dishes hold an array of mushroom hors d'oeuvres. It's all things mushrooms and beautifully rustic.

# MAGRET DUCK BREAST

Duck is one of those foods that either you love or you don't. We would never serve duck as the single entrée for a dinner unless it's a multicourse meal; then if you're not a duck person you have other courses to make you happy. But this is a very delicious dish.

Since duck is a rich meat, we serve very simple vegetables on the side—pencil-thin white and green asparagus roasted with olive oil and sea salt, and baby squash cooked the same way. (Don't cook the squash with the flowers intact; remove them before cooking and use them to garnish the plate.) Flowering sprigs of thyme top the duck.

Magret duck breast is from the Moulard breed of ducks, a cross between the White Pekin and the Muscovy duck. It has a large, plump breast with deeper, richer, almost beefier flavor than the White Pekin that is most common here in the States.

*Serves 4*

---

1 whole Magret duck breast (about 2 pounds)

Coarse salt and freshly ground black pepper

Preheat the oven to 350°F.

Cut the breast into the two lobes and pat dry. With a very sharp knife, score the skin diagonally. Cut all the way through the skin, but take care not to cut into the meat. Season generously with salt and pepper.

Place the breasts skin side down in a cold, heavy-bottomed, ovenproof 10- or 12-inch sauté pan. Set over medium heat and cook until the skin is crispy, 7 to 10 minutes. Turn the breasts over and cook for 1 minute more.

Transfer the pan to the oven and roast for 5 minutes for rare. If you prefer your duck medium-rare or medium, continue roasting for 5 to 10 minutes more, but take care not to overcook.

Let the duck rest for 10 minutes before slicing on the bias.

# RIB EYE STEAKS WITH GRILLED SPRING ONIONS

We prepare this hearty serving of meat simply, with chive butter and grilled spring onions on the side. We fabricated the cutting-board place mats with a small wooden block to hold the steak knife, and added mini bottles of steak sauce to complete the setting. The key to cooking these steaks well is to start with a really hot grill. We prefer to serve a rib eye medium rare.

Note that the steaks need to marinate overnight.

*Serves 4*

3 cups extra-virgin olive oil, plus more for marinating

2 bunches of fresh thyme

8 shallots, minced

1 head of garlic, minced

4 whole boneless rib-eye steaks, about 2 inches thick (1 pound each)

3 bunches of spring onions, halved

Coarse salt and freshly ground black pepper

4 tablespoons Chive Butter (at right)

In a 4-quart container, mix the oil, thyme, shallots and garlic. Submerge the steaks in the oil and marinate in the refrigerator for at least 6 hours or preferably overnight. (The more it marinates, the more tender the meat.)

Toss the spring onions with olive oil to coat and season with salt and pepper.

Bring the meat up to room temperature 1 hour before cooking. When ready to cook, remove the beef from the pan and wipe off the excess oil, garlic, and shallots. Season the meat with salt and pepper.

Heat a grill or grill pan to high and grill the steaks to the desired doneness. For a medium-rare steak, grill the rib eye 3 to 4 minutes on each side. Grill the spring onions very quickly, turning once, just until they are grill marked and soft.

Let the meat rest for 10 minutes. Just before serving (but while the steaks are still hot), spoon 1 tablespoon of chive butter on top of each steak. Serve the grilled onions on the side.

## Chive Butter

*Makes about ½ pound*

½ pound (2 sticks) unsalted butter, softened

1 bunch of fresh chives, finely chopped

Grated zest of 1 lemon

Coarse salt and freshly ground black pepper

In a small bowl, combine the butter, chives, lemon zest, and salt and pepper to taste. Set aside until ready to serve.

# TAGINE SPICED CHICKEN BREAST

When serving chicken, it's important that it doesn't dry out. So one thing that makes this dish successful is the great broth; the other is the spices—paprika, cinnamon, turmeric, ginger, crushed red pepper, and cardamom—that add a very distinctive flavoring. The dish is served in a shallow bowl; you pour the broth in first, then add the vegetables, and place the chicken on top.

Years ago, I learned an important point about chicken. My mother always told me that fat is your enemy, so when I ate chicken at home, it never had any skin on it. However, when you're preparing chicken for special-event dinners that need to be delicious, you must have the skin—but it needs to get really, really crispy. So the trick to making any chicken dish delicious is to sear it in as hot a pan as possible to make the skin as crispy as you can get it.

Note that the chicken needs to marinate overnight.

*Serves 4*

1 2-ounce jar tagine spice

4 or 5 garlic cloves, peeled

Extra-virgin olive oil to make a paste, plus 1 tablespoon for the pan

4 boneless, skin-on chicken breasts

Preserved lemon slices, for garnish

Couscous with Chickpeas, Olives, and Pomegranate (page 168)

Combine the tagine spice and garlic in a food processor. With the motor running, add the oil in small increments until you have a spreadable paste.

Pat the chicken breasts dry with paper towels and place in a baking pan. Smear the tagine-garlic paste over both sides. Cover the pan with plastic wrap and refrigerate overnight.

Bring the chicken up to room temperature at least 30 minutes before cooking. When ready to cook, wipe the chicken clean of all the paste.

Preheat the oven to 350°F.

Heat the 1 tablespoon olive oil in a heavy-bottomed, ovenproof sauté pan over high heat until almost smoking. Carefully add the chicken, skin side down. Cook until the skin is crispy, then flip and cook for 2 to 3 minutes more. Transfer the pan to the oven and roast until cooked through, about 20 minutes.

To serve, spoon some of the pan juices into the bottom of a bowl, add a mound of couscous, and place the chicken on top. Garnish with a slice of preserved lemon.

# Couscous with Chickpeas, Olives, and Pomegranate

*Serves 4*

---

2 cups Israeli couscous (also called pearl couscous)

¼ cup extra-virgin olive oil

3 tablespoons coarse salt, plus more to season

½ cup pitted, halved Castelvetrano olives, or other large green olives

1 cup cooked chickpeas (drained and rinsed if canned)

¼ cup pomegranate seeds

Freshly ground black pepper

Preheat the oven to 350°F.

On a half-sheet pan, toss the couscous with 2 tablespoons of the olive oil and spread in an even layer. Roast until lightly browned, about 10 minutes.

Fill a medium pot with 1 quart water, add the 3 tablespoons salt, and bring to a boil over medium heat. Add the couscous and cook until tender, 8 to 10 minutes. Drain, transfer to a large mixing bowl, and toss with the remaining 2 tablespoons olive oil.

Add the olives, chickpeas, and pomegranate seeds and toss to combine. Season with salt and pepper to taste.

## ADDING COLOR AND TEXTURE TO THE PLATE

When you envision plating a dish, keep an eye out for color. In fall or winter you may be thinking everything brown is okay, but it's nice to add color to the plate. We like to do this with the vegetables, the sauce for the entrée, and the garnish. We also like to have different textures on the plate. It's one reason we top the branzino with toasted panko (see page 137). It adds a nice crunch and a golden brown color to contrast the whiteness of the fish. Watermelon radish is popular in an entrée side dish because it adds both crunch and beautiful color.

White plates make food look the most beautiful. You have a blank slate, and the ingredients themselves add the color. On a very ornate plate, the food can get lost. Sometimes clients have a specific plate in mind, especially for smaller parties in their home where they want to use their own china. So we think about what the color of the plate is and what looks good on it, if we have the option.

As a change of pace, we sometimes use slate gray plates, which make the colors of the food pop. We also like to serve our food on wooden boards, which we cut ourselves. It makes for an unusual presentation.

# CORN CAKES

We serve delicious, light corn cakes (bottom left on page 170) with a sour cream and chive sauce on the side.

*Makes about fifty 2- to 3-inch cakes*

---

½ cup cornmeal

⅓ cup all-purpose flour

1¼ teaspoons coarse salt

3 large eggs

3 large egg yolks

⅓ cup Drawn Butter (page 202), plus more for the griddle

1½ cups roughly chopped fresh corn (can do in a food processor)

½ bunch of fresh chives, chopped (about ½ cup)

Sour Cream and Chive Sauce (at right)

In a large bowl, combine the cornmeal, flour, and salt. In a medium bowl, whisk together the eggs and yolks. Add the butter to the eggs and whisk to combine.

Add the egg mixture to the cornmeal mixture and stir to combine. Stir in the corn and chives.

Heat an electric griddle to 350°F (or a stovetop griddle to medium), and brush the surface with butter.

Drop the batter onto the griddle by spoonfuls, about 1½ inches apart. Let cook until bubbles begin to form on the top and the bottom is golden brown, about 3 minutes. Flip and cook until golden brown on the other side, about 1 minute. Transfer the cooked cakes to a platter.

Bring the griddle back up to temperature, brush the surface with butter, and repeat with the remaining batter. Serve with the sour cream and chive sauce on the side.

## Sour Cream and Chive Sauce

*Makes 1½ cups*

---

½ cup extra-virgin olive oil

1⅓ cups chopped fresh chives

¾ cup sour cream

Combine the oil and chives in a blender or food processor and pulse until smooth. Place the sour cream in a medium bowl and fold in the chive mixture. Cover and chill for at least 1 hour before serving.

**CORN ON THE COB STATION** A buffet of everything corn is a great way to celebrate summer. We have freshly grilled corn with herbed olive oils and salts (Maldon and pink and black Himalayan) for garnish, corn cakes and spicy corn soup shooters (you'll find the recipe for the soup in my first book, *Bite by Bite*), and shaved corn dressed with fresh herbs for those who don't want to eat it off the cob. Having some whole corn jammed into the slats of the table brings the theme of corn to life.

Carts have become a big part of the entertainment at events and we often do a roaming cart where the waiter shaves corn tableside. It's a new take on the old Caesar salad service. People like to see the corn cut right in front of them—it's a show and it emphasizes that the corn is fresh.

# CINNAMON-SUGAR PRETZELS

Pretzels are the perfect item to display on a dessert wall (page 174). With savory, pictured, we love to pair our favorite beers; with sweet, as in this recipe, try Prosecco.

*Makes 20*

| | |
|---|---|
| 1 tablespoon active dry yeast | 3 cups all-purpose flour, plus more for kneading |
| 2 tablespoons light brown sugar | 2 teaspoons coarse salt |
| 1 cup warm (110°F) water | 1 cup granulated sugar |
| 6 tablespoons (¾ stick) unsalted butter, melted, plus more for greasing the bowl | 3 tablespoons ground cinnamon |
| | ¼ cup baking soda |
| | 1 large egg beaten with 1 tablespoon water |

In a large bowl, dissolve the yeast and brown sugar in the warm water. Set aside until foamy, about 10 minutes. Add 2 tablespoons of the melted butter, the flour, and salt and mix to incorporate. Turn out on a lightly floured work surface and knead until a smooth, elastic dough forms. Place the dough in a large greased bowl, turn it to butter all sides, cover with plastic wrap, and let rise until doubled in size, about 1 hour.

Punch down the dough and portion into 1-ounce balls (you should have about 20). Roll the balls into ropes and then twist into pretzel shapes, placing them on a tray as you go. Cover the pretzels with a clean kitchen towel and let rise until puffy, about 20 minutes.

Preheat the oven to 450°F. Line a baking sheet with parchment paper.

Combine the sugar and cinnamon in a wide shallow dish and set aside.

In a large pot over medium heat, bring 6 cups water and the baking soda to a simmer. Working in batches, carefully drop the pretzels in the water and simmer for 15 to 30 seconds, or until they float. Remove with a slotted spoon and place on the prepared baking sheet. Brush lightly on both sides with the egg wash.

Bake for 1 to 2 minutes, or until just beginning to color. Brush quickly with the remaining melted butter and return to the oven to bake until golden brown, about 10 minutes. Brush once more with butter after baking. Toss in the cinnamon-sugar while still warm.

## DESSERT WALLS

Food displays that fill vertical space make for an attractive and user-friendly design. The doughnut wall I dreamed up is a great example. You can create a simple pegboard using plywood and hooks. It works with doughnuts, bagels, soft pretzels, Bundt cakes, and more.

A couple who are regular clients moved from New York City to Brentwood, California, and were having a party for all of their new West Coast friends. As guests left the party, they passed the wall, hung with bagels that we had flown in from H & H Bagels in Manhattan. Everyone could take home an authentic New York bagel.

We introduced this wall to New York (and the world) on the *Today* show at Savannah Guthrie's baby shower, where we used doughnuts and cinnamon-sugar-coated soft pretzels. It also made an appearance at a U.S. State Department event for the American Chef Corps (see page 121), which brings together chefs from all over the country.

We can set up the display in two different ways—as part of a dessert buffet (or as a dessert buffet on its own) or by the front door or just outside the entry as a take-home treat. In either case, we have custom bags with printed stickers available to hold the doughnut or pretzel, since this is not a one-bite item and guests may want to take it home.

I filed and got a U.S. Design Patent on this as I was the first known person to create this idea.

# INDIVIDUAL APPLE TARTE TATINS

Many of our seated dinners feature very classic menus, and this is one of our favorite desserts to finish such a meal. It's very simple to make (especially if you use store-bought puff pastry), and yet people always love it. We take a thin slice from the center of each apple and dry it in the oven to make the garnish. A honeycomb serves as the base for a mini scoop of cinnamon ice cream. We make our own, but it's easy enough to add cinnamon to your favorite brand of store-bought vanilla. Store-bought caramel sauce is a good shortcut for this recipe, too.

*Serves 6*

---

All-purpose flour, for dusting

1 sheet store-bought puff pastry, thawed if frozen

Nonstick cooking spray

6 cooking apples, such as Granny Smith or Cortland

6 tablespoons unsalted butter

1½ cups (packed) light brown sugar

1 tablespoon cinnamon

¾ cup Caramel Sauce (recipe follows)

Dried apple slices, for garnish (optional; see Note)

Preheat the oven to 350°F.

Dust a work surface with flour and unfold the sheet of puff pastry. With a 3-inch round biscuit cutter, cut 6 circles from the dough and lay them out on a baking sheet. Prick them all over with a fork, place another baking sheet on top, and bake until golden brown, about 15 minutes.

Line six 4- or 4½-inch fluted tart pans with removable bottoms with aluminum foil and spray liberally with nonstick spray.

Peel and core the apples (see Note). Slice 3 of the apples into very thin crescents. Fan the slices to cover the bottom of the tart pans.

Cut the remaining apples into small dice and place in a 3-quart, heavy-bottomed saucepan over medium heat, along with the butter, brown sugar, and cinnamon. Cook until the apples are cooked through, 7 to 8 minutes. Let the apples cool slightly, then divide the mixture evenly among the tart pans. Spoon 2 tablespoons of the caramel sauce over the apples in each pan and bake until bubbling and golden, 15 to 20 minutes. Remove from the oven and let cool slightly.

When ready to serve, place a dessert plate on top of each tart. Flip the tart over onto the plate and remove the tart pan and foil. Use the remaining caramel sauce to squeeze over the apples and decorate the plate. Garnish with the dried apple slices, if using.

---

***NOTE***

If you wish to top the tarte tatins with a dried apple slice, cut a thin slice from the center, including the stem, from each of the apples before peeling and coring. Place the apple slices in a bowl of water with the juice of half a lemon and let sit for 30 minutes. Preheat the oven to 200°F. Dry the apple slices well and lay them in a single layer on a parchment-paper-lined baking sheet. Bake for 1 hour, turn, and bake for 1 hour more. Turn off the oven, crack open the door, and let the apples cool in the oven.

# Caramel Sauce

*Makes about 1¾ cups*

2½ cups sugar

1½ cups heavy cream

2½ tablespoons unsalted butter,
  cut into small pieces

1½ ounces dark rum, bourbon, or
  amaretto (optional)

Combine the sugar with ¼ cup water in a 3-quart, heavy-bottomed saucepan over medium heat. Bring to a boil while washing down the sides of the pan with a wet pastry brush. Boil until the sugar caramelizes and turns a dark golden brown, 5 to 7 minutes. Watch carefully, as the caramel can burn very quickly.

Remove the pan from the heat and add the cream slowly and carefully. Whisk to blend. Add the butter and stir with a wooden spoon until the butter is melted and fully combined. Stir in the alcohol, if using.

Store any extra sauce in a tightly sealed jar in the fridge for up to 2 months. Use it as a topping for ice cream or apple pie.

**PERFECT PRESENTATION**

## HAMANTASCHEN CHANDELIER

Hamantaschen are filled cookies traditionally baked during the feast of Purim, which celebrates the victory of the Jews over the evil Persian overlord, Haman. These delicious cookies are a springtime favorite. Hung on an acrylic chandelier, they look like small pieces of stained glass, ready to grab and go. You could use a mobile to hang the cookies from.

# HAMANTASCHEN

The most traditional fillings for these cookies are poppy seed or prune butter, but feel free to use your favorite jam or preserves. Note that the dough needs to chill overnight.

*Makes 30*

---

½ pound (2 sticks) unsalted butter

½ cup sugar

¼ cup honey

¼ teaspoon coarse salt

2 large eggs

2 teaspoons baking powder

½ teaspoon baking soda

3 cups pastry flour

1 cup bread flour

¼ teaspoon pure vanilla extract

Nonstick cooking spray

All-purpose flour, for rolling the dough

2 cups apricot jam, raspberry jam, or Nutella

In the bowl of a stand mixer fitted with the paddle attachment, cream the butter and sugar until pale in color. Add the honey and salt and mix until just combined. Add the eggs one at a time, mixing after each addition.

In a large bowl, combine the baking powder, baking soda, pastry flour, and bread flour. Add the dry ingredients to the wet and mix until just combined. Stir in the vanilla, cover the bowl, and chill the dough in the fridge overnight.

Line two baking sheets with parchment paper and grease with cooking spray.

On a lightly floured surface, roll the dough ⅛ inch thick. Use a 3-inch round cookie cutter to cut circles from the dough. Transfer them to the prepared baking sheets, spacing them about 1 inch apart. Place 1 tablespoon of the desired filling in the center of each circle. Gently fold one edge of the circle up and press it against but not over the filling. Repeat with the other two sides to form a triangle, pinching the seams together. Some of the filling should remain exposed.

When you have formed all the hamentaschen, cover the baking sheets with plastic wrap and freeze for 30 minutes.

Meanwhile, preheat the oven to 350°F.

Bake the hamentaschen until light golden brown, 8 to 10 minutes.

**CHOUX TABLE** The choux table was a great idea that came from our clients Peter and Alex, who spend a lot of time in Europe. They told us about a place in Paris that has all the choux puffs ready and guns filled with different flavors of pastry cream, and they fill the choux to order.

So we set tiny metal rods the size of lollipop sticks into a board and skewered the choux puffs onto the rods. Then we had holes drilled to hold the guns. When a guest comes up to the table, the server asks, "What kind of filling would you like—hazelnut or pistachio?" And the server fills the puff to order. People are drawn to the interactivity.

## EGG MAN

My inspiration for this concept was the well-known restaurateur and hotelier André Balazs, who has what he calls "egg girls" offering fresh eggs from a basket at tableside at the Standard Hotel. The diners can choose their eggs and then have them cooked to order. Our server carries hard-boiled eggs in a beautiful rustic basket (fitted with salt and pepper, too) to guests at breakfast. Sometimes we do this with warm, soft-boiled eggs.

PERFECT PRESENTATION

# GRILLED NECTARINES WITH LEMON-BASIL SORBET

This dessert bursts with summer flavor. Choose just-ripe nectarines and grill the wedges just long enough to mark them. The lemon-basil sorbet adds a not-too-sweet note and the pink grapefruit sauce ties all the flavors together. Many of our clients like a fruit dessert, which we always pair with small chocolates served family style. Every dessert course must have some chocolate!

*Serves 4 to 6*

---

**For the Lemon-Basil Sorbet:**

2 bunches of basil

2 cups freshly squeezed lemon juice

1½ cups sugar

**For the Pink Grapefruit Sauce:**

1 tablespoon cornstarch

2 cups pink grapefruit juice

½ cup sugar

½ vanilla bean, split lengthwise, seeds scraped

4 or 5 ripe but firm nectarines, cut into uniform wedges

**SORBET**

Strip the basil leaves from the stems. Discard the stems and reserve a few very small leaves or any flowering tops for garnish. Crush the leaves with your hands.

In a blender or food processor, pulse the basil with the lemon juice until the basil is broken up into little flecks.

In a medium saucepan, combine the sugar and 3 cups water. Bring to a simmer over medium heat and cook, stirring, until the sugar dissolves and a syrup is formed. Let the sugar syrup cool completely, then add to the lemon and basil mixture in the blender. Pulse just long enough to combine.

Taste and add more sugar if desired. Pour the sorbet into an ice cream maker and churn according to the manufacturer's directions. Transfer to a metal pan, cover with plastic wrap, and place in the freezer until ready to serve.

**GRAPEFRUIT SAUCE**

In a small bowl, mix the cornstarch with 1 tablespoon water to form a paste. In a medium saucepan over medium heat, bring the pink grapefruit juice, sugar, and vanilla bean to a boil. Remove the pan from the heat and whisk in the cornstarch paste. Set the pan over medium-low heat and cook until the mixture thickens. Discard the vanilla bean and transfer the sauce to a bowl to cool.

**NECTARINES**

Heat a grill or a grill pan to high. Place the nectarines on the grates and grill quickly—for only a few seconds—on both sides, just to achieve grill marks on the fruit. (The wedges can easily overcook and become too soft to eat.)

**ASSEMBLE**

Drizzle a spoonful of the grapefruit sauce on the plate, followed by 5 nectarine wedges. Add a scoop or quenelle of the lemon-basil sorbet and garnish with small basil leaves and/or basil flowers.

# STRAWBERRY SHORTCAKE

This is my take on a classic dessert that takes advantage of the very short season when local strawberries are in the market. My version gets a lift from the use of lemon cake, which adds a nice, citrusy tang to offset the sweetness of the strawberries. We like the simplicity of this dish and, while it's easy to make, it yields big accolades when served.

*Serves 6*

---

**For the Strawberries:**

1 pint strawberries

3 tablespoons sugar

Grated zest of ½ lemon

½ vanilla bean, split lengthwise, seeds scraped

2 tablespoons Grand Marnier

**For the Lemon Cake:**

8 tablespoons (1 stick) unsalted butter, plus more for greasing the pans

1 cup sugar

2 large eggs

½ teaspoon pure vanilla extract

1⅔ cups all-purpose flour

½ teaspoon baking powder

½ teaspoon baking soda

¼ teaspoon coarse salt

½ cup sour cream

2 tablespoons milk

Grated zest of 1 lemon

**For the Whipped Cream:**

2 cups heavy cream

1 teaspoon pure vanilla extract

3 tablespoons confectioners' sugar

Wild strawberries, left whole for garnish

**STRAWBERRIES**

Clean and quarter the strawberries and place in a medium bowl. Add the sugar, lemon zest, vanilla bean, and Grand Marnier and gently stir to combine. Set aside to macerate at room temperature for 1 hour.

**CAKE**

Preheat the oven to 325°F. Grease three small (5¾ × 3-inch) loaf pans.

In the bowl of a stand mixer fitted with the paddle attachment, cream the butter and sugar together until fluffy and light in color. Add the eggs and vanilla and mix until incorporated, scraping down the sides of the bowl as needed. Sift the flour, baking powder, baking soda, and salt into a large bowl and add all at once to the creamed mixture. Add the sour cream, milk, and lemon zest and mix until just incorporated. Do not overmix.

Divide the batter evenly among the prepared loaf pans, filling each about halfway, and bake for 30 minutes, until a toothpick inserted in the center comes out clean.

**WHIPPED CREAM**

Meanwhile, in the bowl of a stand mixer fitted with the whisk attachment, combine the cream, vanilla, and confectioners' sugar. Whisk to medium peaks.

**SERVE**

Slice the cakes into twelve ½-inch slices (you will have extra slices; save them for another use). Place 2 slices on each plate, slightly staggered. Spoon a large dollop of whipped cream onto one side of the cake slices and top with the macerated strawberries and a garnish of small wild strawberries.

**FRUIT TREES** I like hanging fruit from trees for guests to pick. We've created many variations on the theme—we've used live trees, wooden trees, and acrylic trees. Sometimes the trees are in the active area of an event and sometimes we position them close to the door, so that when people leave they can take home a piece of caramel fruit. In that case, we have little bags handy. We have also set the full-size trees on buffets and used them for hanging cookies. It's a very dramatic display.

The apples and pears are given a more substantial stem and leaf, and then dipped in caramel. The coatings are shaved coconut, pistachio, bacon, and candied ginger.

## FRUIT TOWERS

Our clients often request fruit on a buffet. *Croque-N-bouche* towers as well as the Moroccan markets with their pyramids of spices are the inspiration for this fruit look. You can pick the melon balls right off the tower. A mix of unusual vessels hold honey and other sauces—the effect is exotic and glamorous.

## STRAWBERRY BUFFET

The strawberry buffet was originally designed for a wedding that would take place in a rustic setting on a horse farm. The idea was that everything on the table would include strawberries, and down the middle of the table would be strawberry plants with strawberries on the stems. My mom always had strawberry pots and strawberry plants in the garden.

Anyone who gets through winter dreaming of those first ripe berries knows the season for local strawberries—the sweetest and best kind—is excruciatingly short. I found out after I had promised this display that we had missed the local season by about a month. We called all over the country and despite the promise that price was no object, I was told, "You can't bribe Mother Nature." So we grew them ourselves, forcing them so they would bear fruit in time for the event. We had strawberry plants all over the office, and people came in on the weekends to water them. We had to transport them carefully so that the fruit wouldn't fall from the stems. Now, when we do this display outside of the local strawberry season, we wire individual berries onto the plants to make a lush and fruit-filled display.

The strawberry shortcake is a miniature version of the dessert on page 184, and the recipe for the mini strawberry-rhubarb pies can be found in my first book, *Bite by Bite*. Mini strawberry milkshakes and fresh strawberries complete the service.

# FAMILY STYLE

—

*Entertaining Family
and Friends*

**I love to serve food family style, with large platters of food placed on the table to be passed and shared by all.** This type of service is very popular even at large seated dinners because guests become more engaged with the food—and one another. You pass the platter to the person seated at your left, perhaps holding the dish while they serve themselves. Maybe you serve the food to them. Suddenly you're connected and having conversation over food.

At home, a family-style dinner is an antidote to our grab-and-go lifestyle— a more intimate way to engage family and friends over a meal. It's a casual way to entertain, but it's also beautiful because the food is the focus of the table. Family-style meals aren't the time to pull out the good china, unless you want to. Choose vintage serving bowls, casual dinnerware—maybe even colanders. Don't worry about elaborate centerpieces; they only hinder the conversation. If there's room on the table, you may choose to add a simple, inexpensive flower arrangement, but you don't really need it because the food alone is so lovely.

I've designed these menus to serve six people, but they may easily be adapted for a larger crowd. These are complete menus, but you don't have to make every dish—and you may want to mix and match from one menu to another, or add in your own family's favorites. That's the beauty of family-style dining—there are no rules.

# BREAKFAST AT HOME

Breakfast is one of my favorite meals for entertaining. On Nantucket, where we spend many weekends, we often have people over for breakfast. In the summer, everyone's schedules are super busy: evenings are often booked with parties and events, and weekends get consumed by the myriad demands on people's time. Having people over for breakfast starts the day off with something social but quick, about an hour spent around the table with friends or just family and houseguests.

Broil the grapefruits first and spoon up the berries, then make the waffles and toasts. Mash your avocado close to serving, as it will turn brown if it sits. Make the eggs last, so they won't be overcooked.

*Serves 6*

---

**On the menu:**

Avocado Toast (page 196)

Soft-Boiled Eggs with Toast Soldiers (page 197)

Cinnamon Raisin Waffles (page 197)

Broiled grapefruit halves

Fresh mixed berries in season

Hot and iced coffee

Grapefruit juice

# AVOCADO TOAST

You want avocados that are tender but not quite as soft as those you might use for guacamole. The ripeness of the avocados is important to this dish!

---

6 slices hearty whole-grain
  bread

¼ cup extra-virgin olive oil

3 just-ripe avocados

Juice of 1 lemon

Sea salt and freshly ground
  black pepper

Toast the bread in a toaster or a 350°F oven until light brown and crunchy, about 5 minutes. Brush each slice with 1 teaspoon of the olive oil.

With a sharp paring knife, cut the avocados in half lengthwise and remove the pits. Scoop out the flesh and place in a large bowl. Sprinkle with a few drops of lemon juice. With a large wooden spoon, lightly mash the avocados, keeping the mixture chunky.

Mound some of the chunky avocado mixture onto each slice of toast, using a spoon or small spatula. Sprinkle with salt and pepper and drizzle with more olive oil and a few drops of lemon juice.

Serve the avocado toast immediately, family style, with various garnishes (at right) in bowls on the table.

### Some of Our Favorite Garnishes for Avocado Toast

*A good avocado is delicious on its own, but it also pairs well with many flavors. Consider color, texture, and flavor when choosing accompaniments.*

Maldon sea salt

Crumbled bacon

Quartered heirloom cherry tomatoes, preferably in different colors

Crumbled feta cheese or queso fresco

Grilled corn kernels tossed with minced Serrano peppers and lime juice

Thinly sliced or julienned radishes

Julienne of kale or escarole

Chopped scallions and capers

Toasted pine nuts and chopped sun-dried tomatoes

Toasted pistachios and pistachio oil for drizzling

Toasted sesame seeds and sesame oil for drizzling

Chopped fresh herbs like mint, parsley, cilantro, dill, and marjoram

Freshly ground coriander and cumin seeds

# SOFT-BOILED EGGS WITH TOAST SOLDIERS

Egg cups are essential here so that you can easily dip your toast soldiers into the yolk.

---

6 large eggs

4 tablespoons (½ stick) unsalted butter

½ loaf brioche bread, thickly sliced and cut into ½-inch sticks

½ loaf pumpernickel bread, thickly sliced and cut into ½-inch sticks

Place the eggs in a medium saucepan with 1 quart water. Bring the water to a boil over medium heat and cook the eggs for 6 to 7 minutes. Transfer them immediately to egg cups and crack open the tops.

While the eggs are cooking, melt half the butter in a 10- or 12-inch skillet over medium heat. Working in batches, add the bread to the skillet and toast on each side until golden brown and crispy, 3 to 4 minutes per side. Melt the remaining butter and repeat with the remaining bread.

# CINNAMON RAISIN WAFFLES

We've reproduced the flavor of everyone's favorite breakfast bread in the form of a waffle. Dusted with confectioners' sugar and cinnamon, there's no need for syrup.

*Makes 6 to 8*

---

2 large eggs

1¾ cups buttermilk

8 tablespoons (1 stick) unsalted butter, melted

2 teaspoons pure vanilla extract

2 cups pastry flour

2 tablespoons granulated sugar

2 teaspoons baking powder

1 teaspoon baking soda

1 teaspoon coarse salt

3 teaspoons ground cinnamon

½ cup confectioners' sugar

½ cup raisins

Heat a nonstick waffle iron according to the manufacturer's directions.

In a large bowl, beat together the eggs, buttermilk, melted butter, and vanilla. In a medium bowl, whisk together the flour, granulated sugar, baking powder, baking soda, salt, and 1 teaspoon of the cinnamon. Add the wet ingredients to the dry and combine just until smooth.

In a small bowl, mix together the remaining 2 teaspoons cinnamon and the confectioners' sugar.

Pour ¼ to ⅓ cup batter into the waffle iron. Do not fill the iron completely; the waffles should look free-form and rustic. Dot the waffles with the raisins. Close the lid and bake until done, 3 to 4 minutes. Repeat with the remaining batter and raisins. Sprinkle immediately with the cinnamon sugar and serve.

# FAMILY-STYLE CLAMBAKE

The clambake to me is one of the most all-American staples of the season. Colanders are a fun way to serve this meal; they're iconic, and it's nice to see them repurposed.

This is a simple meal to prepare. You can purchase the lobsters cooked if you like, and stop by the local bakery to pick up the corn muffins. Light the grill (or a grill pan) to get char marks on the chorizo and the lemon halves—a great look without a lot of trouble. The sauces for dunking the clams and lobster can be made well ahead of time, and you can prepare the seafood, corn, and beans while the potatoes are cooking.

Rosé is the go-to for summer, but I also love serving craft beer in a growler. It feels like it's straight from the brewer.

*Serves 6*

---

**On the Menu:**

4 whole 1½-pound lobsters, steamed (see page 125)

Steamed Littleneck Clams (page 200)

Chorizo sausage, cut on the bias and grilled

Corn on the cob

Salt-Baked Potatoes (page 200)

Green Beans and Yellow Wax Beans (page 201)

Corn muffins

Roasted Red Pepper Sauce (page 201)

Pesto (page 202)

Drawn Butter (page 202)

6 lemons, halved

# PESTO

*Makes about 2½ cups*

2½ cups basil leaves

¼ cup freshly squeezed
  lemon juice

2 garlic cloves

¼ cup pine nuts, toasted

3 tablespoons grated
  Parmesan cheese

Pinch of dried red
  pepper flakes

1½ cups extra-virgin
  olive oil

Coarse salt and freshly
  ground black pepper

In a blender or food processor, combine the basil, lemon juice, and garlic and pulse until coarsely chopped. Add the pine nuts, cheese, and red pepper flakes. Pulse on low until combined, then increase the speed to medium. Slowly stream in the olive oil until the sauce just begins to come together. Season with salt and pepper to taste and serve.

Store any leftover pesto in the fridge for up to 3 weeks, or freeze for up to 6 months.

# DRAWN BUTTER

The classic accompaniment to lobster, unsalted butter is heated slowly so that any moisture evaporates and the solids separate, leaving clear liquid butter. Store any leftover butter in a tightly covered container in the refrigerator and use it for cooking. Clarified (drawn) butter, or ghee, has a much higher smoke point than solid butter.

*Makes 1⅓ cups*

1 pound (4 sticks)
  unsalted butter

Place the butter in a small saucepan over medium-low heat. Let the butter melt slowly, skimming off and discarding the white foam that rises to the surface. When the butter has completely melted and separated, carefully ladle the clear golden liquid into a serving ramekin, leaving behind any milk solids at the bottom of the pan.

# MOULES FRITES FOR A CROWD

Moules frites, or steamed mussels with French fries, is a great example of how you don't need that many dishes to make a memorable meal. This menu always evokes memories for me of many different wonderful meals enjoyed at a variety of French bistros. Mussels steamed in garlic and wine, twice-fried frites, a simple salad, and crusty bread to sop up all the broth makes for a great simple summer meal. Prince Edward Island (PEI) mussels are readily available and of consistently good quality. Whatever kind of mussels you choose, be sure to debeard and scrub them well. We follow the Belgian method of "blanching" the potatoes in oil and then freezing them for four hours before deep-frying to get the crispiest frites, so be sure to allow for that time in your cooking schedule. You can also freeze the blanched potatoes for up to a month ahead.

*Serves 6*

---

**On the menu:**

Mussels Steamed in Garlic and Wine (page 206)

Frites (page 206)

Herb Aioli (page 207)

Salad of Baby Red Lettuce and Frisée with Sherry Vinaigrette (page 207)

Creamy Lemon Butter Sauce (page 208)

Sourdough Crostini (page 208)

# CREAMY LEMON BUTTER SAUCE

This delicious sauce is perfect for dunking both the mussels and the crostini.

*Makes about 3 cups*

---

2 cups dry white wine

4 shallots, minced

2 pounds (8 sticks) cold unsalted butter, cut into cubes

¼ cup heavy cream

Coarse salt

In a small saucepan over medium heat, combine the wine and shallots and reduce until only ¼ cup of liquid remains. Remove the pan from the heat and slowly whisk in the butter, a few cubes at a time. Once the butter is completely incorporated, whisk in the heavy cream and salt to taste. Serve immediately or hold in a warm space.

# SOURDOUGH CROSTINI

A good, crusty sourdough loaf is key here. These crostini are great for eating on their own or sopping up all the delicious seafood juices.

---

1 long sourdough baguette, sliced on a long bias

2 cups extra-virgin olive oil

¼ cup chopped fresh basil

¼ cup chopped fresh flat-leaf parsley

Coarse salt

Preheat the oven to 350°F. Line a baking sheet with parchment paper.

Lay the bread slices in a single layer on the prepared baking sheet. In a small bowl, whisk together the olive oil, basil, parsley, and salt. Brush the herb oil on top of the bread slices.

Toast in the oven until the bread is golden brown but the center is still fairly soft, 10 to 12 minutes. Serve immediately with the mussels.

# TACO NIGHT

Tacos seem to be one of the most popular foods around these days. Lots of restaurants specialize in them and "Taco Tuesdays" have become a weekly standard. It's really easy to set out an assortment of fillings and let everyone make their own tacos. Pair them with a great tequila and ice-cold Mexican beer in bottles and you have a terrific meal for family and friends.

The sauces and salsas can be made in advance, and the chicken can be made a day or two ahead as well. The steak needs to be marinated overnight, but it cooks quickly, as does the fish.

*Serves 6*

---

**On the menu:**

Chile-Rubbed Pulled Chicken
  (page 212)

Crispy Roasted Cod (page 212)

Grilled Hanger Steak (page 213)

Mexican Corn on the Cob
  (page 213)

Tortillas

Roasted chile peppers

Avocado

Mango salsa

Pico de gallo

Hot sauce

Thinly sliced scallions

Lime wedges

Mexican beer

Tequila on ice

# VIETNAMESE DINNER

Like tacos, this meal really adds the make-it-yourself aspect to the family style, this time with lettuce leaves instead of tortillas. This meal looks exotic but requires little effort—there are a lot of condiments in addition to the fillings for the wraps. The showstopper is the whole fish. It's easy to make and people love it. Many people have never had a whole fish, and it can be nice to introduce family and friends to the cuisine of another region.

This meal features flavorful sauces for dipping or adding to the lettuce wraps. They can be made a few days ahead and refrigerated. These sauces would pair equally well with any roasted meat—and its visually attractive to have lots of small bowls filled with colorful ingredients dotting the table.

*Serves 6*

---

**On the menu:**

Whole Fried Red Snapper
(page 216)

Lemongrass Ginger Chicken
(page 216)

Grilled Shrimp on Sugarcane
Skewers (page 217)

1 or 2 heads of butter lettuce

Green Papaya Salad (page 217)

Chili Fish Sauce (page 218)

Sriracha-Lime Sauce (page 218)

Peanut Sauce (page 218)

Pickled Carrots and Daikon
Radish (page 219)

Lychee and Lime Spritzer
(page 219)

# PICNIC ON THE LAWN

A picnic with family and friends is all about being easy. These sandwiches are homemade, but they could just as easily be purchased at the local gourmet shop. Add a tray of your favorite cheeses and charcuterie, fruits and vegetables in season, and a good loaf of bread, and you have a delicious array to spread on a blanket in the park. A chilled bottle of rosé is the perfect complement to the meal. The key to a stress-free picnic is portability, so we serve the panna cotta dessert in lidded jars to ensure there'll be no spills en route.

*Serves 6*

---

**On the menu:**

| | |
|---|---|
| Avocado BLTs on ciabatta rolls | Bresaola |
| Fresh radishes | Cornichons |
| Fresh figs | Crusty baguette |
| Sliced melon | Water with lemon and fresh mint |
| A selection of cheeses | Rosé |
| Prosciutto | Panna cotta jars |

# BARS, CARTS, AND SPECIALTY DRINKS

—

*Fun and Unique*
*Service Scenarios*

With the rise of the craft cocktail, specialty drinks have become more and more important at events. Bar service used to be (and still predominantly is) glasses placed attractively on the tabletop, with a few bottles of alcohol and a few small bottles of soda. You put your condiments in a glass, and you're done. You might have some specialty drinks in pitchers toward the rear of the bar.

The bartender may tell the guest what the specials are, or there might be a menu card on the table. We put these vivid specialty drinks in attractive carafes or decanters, floating above the table on a riser. We do that by making an acrylic board with feet and placing it on the bar, perched above the glasses. Your eye is drawn to the board, and you're thinking, What is that? In this way the specialty drinks become the decor of the bar.

We also put chilling boxes on the end of the bar to chill the wine and Champagne and let guests see what we are offering. These are square boxes similar to a wine bucket, which could also be used. But, most important, the specialty drink is front and center. We started that years ago and now it's become the standard.

## FIREBALL CART

**PERFECT PRESENTATION**

Fireball, the cinnamon-flavored whiskey-based liqueur, has become popular among young groups. The recipe for the classic version of the cocktail is on page 227. The graphics on the bottle are part of its appeal, so we replicate them on the cart and decorate the edges with sparklers. We put labels on small glass bottles and have fireball candy stoppers on top. We drill a hole through the stopper and insert a straw. Roll one of these carts around a party after dinner and the message is loud and clear: "Please stay and let's have fun!" There are many variations on this cart, including one for kids with a nonalcoholic fireball-candy spritzer.

FIREBALL

RED     HOT

CINNAMON WHISKY

**MOSCOW MULE CART** Moscow Mules have been around since the 1940s. They have become popular again, particularly when served in copper mugs, which I first discovered with my son while skiing out west. I like to serve them on a cart with both full-size and mini mugs, so a guest can have half a drink or even a quarter of a drink—they don't have to make a full commitment! Sometimes we bring the carts out following dinner, if the client wants the party to continue afterward.

# MOSCOW MULE

*Makes 1*

---

1½ ounces vodka

½ ounce freshly
squeezed lime juice

½ cup ginger beer

Crystallized ginger, for
garnish

Mint sprig, for garnish

Lime wedge, for garnish

Mix the vodka and lime juice in a copper mug or
highball glass. Add ice and top with the ginger
beer, stirring once. Garnish with crystallized
ginger, a sprig of mint, and a lime wedge.


# FIREBALL COCKTAIL

*Makes 1*

---

½ ounce Fireball
cinnamon whiskey

½ cup Angry Orchard
cider

In an ice-filled shaker, combine the Fireball and
the cider. Shake well and pour into a rocks glass
filled with ice.


# BLOODY MARY

*Makes 4*

---

1 quart tomato juice

3 tablespoons freshly
squeezed lemon juice

½ teaspoon
Worcestershire sauce

1½ teaspoons Tabasco
sauce

2 tablespoons freshly
grated horseradish

½ teaspoon celery seed

½ teaspoon ground
cumin

½ teaspoon ground
coriander

1 cup vodka

4 small celery ribs with
leaves, for garnish

Combine the tomato juice, lemon juice,
Worcestershire sauce, Tabasco, horseradish,
celery seed, cumin, coriander, and vodka in a
pitcher and stir vigorously to mix well. Fill four
highball glasses with ice, pour in the Bloody
Mary mix, and garnish with the celery ribs.

**BLOODY MARY BAR** Bloody Marys these days are all about the garnishes, so we provide everything that anyone could want to add to their glass. Yes, there's the traditional celery, but also shrimp, fried oysters, watermelon radishes, asparagus, artichoke hearts, capers, saffron threads, cornichons, cured olives, and celery salt. We often provide pitchers of plain tomato and other juices and let people mix their own Bloodies, providing hot sauce and clam juice on the side. It's like a bar buffet.

PERFECT PRESENTATION

### BACON AND BOURBON BUFFET

My dad had a sailboat we could cruise on and the "refrigerator" was an ice box cooled by a big block of ice. When it was time to make himself a drink, he would just take an ice pick and break off a chunk. With all the interest in mixology and its emphasis on clear ice, it can be very expensive to purchase all those fancy ice cubes. Plus that's been done. My new thing is to buy a big block of ice and let guests chip off their own with an ice pick. It makes for a great design element.

Here we're doing a tasting of both premium bourbons and a variety of bacon types: duck bacon, lamb bacon, chicken pancetta, and Mangalitsa pork bacon.

**WINE STAND**  A large-format wine bottle is like an event all by itself. The bottle pictured here is called a jeroboam: at 4.5 liters, it's equivalent to six standard 750-ml bottles. The size draws people over and creates a special, festive atmosphere. If you had ten nice bottles of red wine sitting on a table, they won't create excitement the way a large-format bottle does. Even pouring from it is entertaining. Here, we display it the way one might a sculpture, with its own pedestal, because it deserves that kind of attention. We offer these at cocktail time, during dinner if it is a buffet, or after dinner.

PERFECT PRESENTATION

**ICE SHOTS** I often do a drink moment at the end of the meal to indicate that the party is to continue. Nothing says more clearly that the host wants you to stay than bringing out shots. We don't ask the guests; we simply bring out three shots and place them at 12:00 above their plates. In this case, it's a shot of Hendrick's gin with cucumber, a Vesper with a lemon twist, and a classic martini with an olive. It brings the energy of the party up from the slower pace of dinner.

PERFECT PRESENTATION

**SNOWBALLS** A tray of these beautiful snow-balls greeted guests at the door to a winter wonderland–themed party. The tray was laid with shaved ice to hold the snowballs in place. No gloves were needed—we carefully measured the amount of the drink to be commensurate with the time that a guest could comfortably hold the snowball. It's a quick-drink moment that served as a fun start to the evening.

## MARGARITA BAR

This is a twist on a tequila bar, where the guests can taste different types of tequila. The margarita bar is all about the drinks themselves—they really become the whole focus. The fresh fruits identify the types of margaritas: pomegranate, lime, and grapefruit. And although we've already rimmed the glasses with salt, the bowls of salt are part of the look.

**JALAPEÑO MARGARITAS** This is my favorite margarita—a classic made with jalapeño simple syrup. The kick of spice is a great flavor boost. We serve them with a garnish of sugar coated chile peppers. Garnishes that identify the drink enhance the visual display with specialty cocktails.

# JALAPEÑO MARGARITAS

*Makes 4*

---

¾ cup tequila

1 cup freshly squeezed
lime juice

1 cup Jalapeño Simple
Syrup (recipe follows)

Candied Chile Peppers,
for garnish (recipe
follows)

In a large pitcher, combine the tequila, lime
juice, jalapeño simple syrup, and 1 cup water.
Stir to mix well. Pour over ice into a double old-
fashioned glass and garnish with a candied chile
pepper to serve.

---

### JALAPEÑO SIMPLE SYRUP

Combine 2 cups sugar, 2 cups water, and 2 jalapeños,
cut in half, in a small, heavy-bottomed saucepan. Cook
over medium heat, stirring occasionally, until the
sugar has dissolved completely. Remove from the heat
and let cool. Strain into a lidded jar. Simple syrup will
keep in the fridge for up to 1 month.

### CANDIED CHILE PEPPERS

In a small, heavy-bottomed saucepan over medium
heat, cook 8 small chile peppers in 1 cup plain simple
syrup (at right) for 10 to 15 minutes. Remove the chiles
from the syrup (which you can reserve for another use)
and dry on a cooling rack overnight. Toss the chiles
in granulated sugar just before using. Cut a slit in the
pepper to hang it on the rim of the glass.

# CLASSIC MARGARITA

*Makes 4*

---

¾ cup tequila

¼ cup Grand Marnier

1 cup freshly squeezed
lime juice

1 cup Simple Syrup
(recipe follows)

In a large pitcher, combine the tequila, Grand
Marnier, lime juice, simple syrup, and 1 cup water.
Stir to mix well, and pour over ice in a tall glass
(such as a double old-fashioned) to serve.

---

### SIMPLE SYRUP

Combine 2 cups sugar and 2 cups water in a small,
heavy-bottomed saucepan. Cook over medium heat,
stirring occasionally, until the sugar has dissolved
completely. Remove from the heat and let cool. Simple
syrup will keep in the fridge for up to 1 month.

**GRANITA CART** Carts are becoming very popular—it's like the buffet comes to you. We bring this granita cart out after dinner, when people might be dancing and looking for something light and refreshing. We often do alcohol pairings with it as well. The cart looks pretty with all the toppings, but the granitas are really delicious on their own.

**MINI AFFOGATO** The mini affogato is a great dessert to kick off after-dinner festivities: it's a coffee, it's a dessert—it's both. We serve these in mini stemless glasses for an attractive presentation. We put a scoop of frozen ice cream in the warm espresso, timed so that the ice cream hasn't all melted but is still drinkable by the time it's served. We do put a little spoon with it, but you don't really need one—most people drink it like a shot. The rich espresso and creamy vanilla are a simple but great combination.

# BEE'S KNEES

Some say this Prohibition-era cocktail was devised to mask the taste of bathtub gin, but today it's a delicious and refreshing drink for any occasion. Peter and Alex (see page 107) had us use ostrich eggs as glasses to serve this cocktail at their thoughtful wedding. The garnish was a sprig of flowering lavender and a piece of honeycomb. We glued white plastic rings to the bottom of the eggs so guests could set them down.

*Makes 2*

---

8 ounces gin

½ cup freshly squeezed lemon juice

½ cup Honey Simple Syrup (recipe follows)

Combine the gin, lemon juice, and honey simple syrup in an ice-filled shaker. Shake vigorously until chilled and strain into chilled coupe glasses.

---

### *HONEY SIMPLE SYRUP*

In a medium saucepan over medium heat, bring ½ cup water to a boil. Reduce the heat to low, add ½ cup lavender honey, and stir to combine. Let cool. Pour into a jar or bottle with a secure top and refrigerate for up to 1 month.

# POMEGRANATE AND BLACKBERRY MARTINI

This is the perfect cocktail for Halloween or any time you want to serve something dramatic and delicious. Serve it in a skull bottle, as we do on page 53, or in a shot glass.

*Makes 4 full-size or 24 mini*

---

1 cup blackberries

2 cups pomegranate juice

½ cup vodka

Blend the blackberries and pomegranate juice in a blender. After completely blended, strain through a fine-mesh strainer. Combine the vodka and strained juice in an ice-filled cocktail shaker. Shake and serve neat in classic martini glasses or funnel into mini crystal skull bottles with red straws (see Sources, page 251).

## THE CHEMISTRY BAR

People look to me for entertaining ways to
serve. This is a chemistry bar—a bit of a play
on the artisan mixologists who make their
drinks with a lot of fancy equipment and eye
droppers. There are mixed drinks in all the
beakers, and we've added some interesting
garnishes, like the cucumber pearls and
microgreens. Then we activate it with dry-
ice smoke.

# Acknowledgments

I want to thank Beth, Trish, Adam, and Ken, who make our parties happen.
I am grateful for Doris Cooper at Clarkson Potter for her continued support;
Amanda Englander, my editor; Ian Dingman, who designed the book; as well
as Ada Yonenaka, Philip Leung, Jana Branson, and Carolyn Gill. It was great
to again have the photography and food styling talents of Con Poulos. It was
a pleasure to work with Marisa Bulzone as my cowriter. I also want to thank
Ayesha Patel and Kate Berry, and Kevin Sharkey, who always connects me to
such great talent. And there are so many more who are part of our team who
contribute daily—my thanks to all of them.

# Sources

My team and I spend a lot of time searching out the perfect platters, mini mugs, and serving ware, not to mention key ingredients like wasabi caviar and truffles, that absolutely make a dish. This list details the sources I turn to when I need something to make a party or a dish special.

## EQUIPMENT AND SERVING WARE

**Acrylic containers, ice buckets, and sheets**
clearlyacrylic.com
877-360-4163

**Chinese take-out boxes, mini sand pails, plastic 1½-inch-high shot glasses**
orientaltrading.com
800-875-8480

**Pastry tips**
pastrysampler.com
760-440-9171

**Cookie cutters**
thecookiecuttershop.com
360-652-3295

**Dishers**
kitchenconservatory.com
866-862-CHEF (2433)

**Eggshells**
theeggeryplace.com
972-241-4379

etsy.com/shop/NakedEggs

**Mini cups, mugs, and glasses**
giantpartystore.com
866-244-1169

**Mini copper mugs**
beau-coup.com
877-988-2328

**Mini Popsicle molds and sticks**
e-store.worldofgelato.com
877-2GELATO (243-5286)

zokuhome.com

**Glass domes and matching trays**
crateandbarrel.com
800-967-6696

potterybarn.com
888-779-5176

**Mini loaf pans**
webstaurantstore.com
717-392-7472

3¼ × 5¾-inch loaf pan (by Chicago Metallic)
kitchenkapers.com
800-455-5567

**Mandoline**
(we like the Benriner brand)
surlatable.com
800-243-0852

**Pallet holder for cones**
pastryitems.com
443-417-8854

**Scallop shells**
seashellcity.com
888-743-5524

seashellsupply.com

**Mini skull bottles and short drinking straws**
barproducts.com
800-256-6396

**Mini tart pans**
kitchenconservatory.com

**Wooden forks, paper cones, paper sandwich bags, cone pallets, mini plates and serving cups, and serving stands**
previninc.com
888-285-9547

restaurantware.com
800-851-9273

**Tables, chairs, kitchen equipment, china, glasses, flatware, and more**
LuxeEventRentals.com
NY/Miami: 718-629-6909

partyrentalltd.com
201-727-4700

**Custom, print-on-demand fabric, wallpaper, and gift wrap**
spoonflower.com
919-886-7885

## INGREDIENTS

**Concord Foods Caramel Apple Kit**
concordfoods.com
508-580-1700

**Caviar and truffles**
American paddlefish caviar
paramountcaviar.com
800-99CAVIAR (992-2842)

**Crawfish**
klcrawfishfarms.com

**Edible candy wrappers**
molecularrecipes.com

**Foie gras and Magret duck**
dartagnan.com
800-327-8246

**Miniature (50 ml) bottles Maker's Mark**
beerliquors.com
877-624-1982

**Vegetables**
chefs-garden.com
800-289-4644

# Index

Copyright © 2017 by **PETER CALLAHAN**
Photography copyright © 2017
by **CON POULOS**

All rights reserved.
Published in the United States by
**CLARKSON POTTER/PUBLISHERS**, an imprint
of the **CROWN PUBLISHING GROUP**,
a division of **PENGUIN RANDOM HOUSE LLC**,
New York.
crownpublishing.com
clarksonpotter.com

**CLARKSON POTTER** is a trademark and
**POTTER** with colophon is a registered
trademark of **PENGUIN RANDOM HOUSE LLC**.

Library of Congress Cataloging-in-
Publication Data
is available upon request.

ISBN 978-0-553-45971-5
eBook ISBN 978-0-553-45972-2

Printed in China

Book and cover design by **IAN DINGMAN**
Cover photography by **CON POULOS**

10 9 8 7 6 5 4 3 2 1

First Edition